ZEPHANIAH

and

HAGGAI

J. Vernon McGee

THOMAS NELSON PUBLISHERS

Nashville • Atlanta • London • Vancouver

Published in Nashville, Tennessee, by Thomas Nelson, Inc.

Scripture quotations are from the KING JAMES VERSION of the Bible.

Library of Congress Cataloging-in-Publication Data

McGee, J. Vernon (John Vernon), 1904–1988
   [Thru the Bible with J. Vernon McGee]
   Thru the Bible commentary series / J. Vernon McGee.
     p.   cm.
   Reprint. Originally published: Thru the Bible with J. Vernon McGee. 1975.
   Includes bibliographical references.
   ISBN 0-7852-1034-2 (TR)
   ISBN 0-7852-1094-6 (NRM)
   1. Bible—Commentaries. I. Title.
BS491.2.M37   1991
220.7′7—dc20
          90–41340
          CIP

PRINTED IN MEXICO

12 13 - 05

CONTENTS

ZEPHANIAH

HAGGAI

PREFACE

The radio broadcasts of the Thru the Bible Radio five-year program were transcribed, edited, and published first in single-volume paperbacks to accommodate the radio audience.

There has been a minimal amount of further editing for this publication. Therefore, these messages are not the word-for-word recording of the taped messages which went out over the air. The changes were necessary to accommodate a reading audience rather than a listening audience.

These are popular messages, prepared originally for a radio audience. They should not be considered a commentary on the entire Bible in any sense of that term. These messages are devoid of any attempt to present a theological or technical commentary on the Bible. Behind these messages is a great deal of research and study in order to interpret the Bible from a popular rather than from a scholarly (and too-often boring) viewpoint.

We have definitely and deliberately attempted "to put the cookies on the bottom shelf so that the kiddies could get them."

The fact that these messages have been translated into many languages for radio broadcasting and have been received with enthusiasm reveals the need for a simple teaching of the whole Bible for the masses of the world.

I am indebted to many people and to many sources for bringing this volume into existence. I should express my especial thanks to my secretary, Gertrude Cutler, who supervised the editorial work; to Dr. Elliott R. Cole, my associate, who handled all the detailed work with the publishers; and finally, to my wife Ruth for tenaciously encouraging me from the beginning to put my notes and messages into printed form.

Solomon wrote, ". . . of making many books there is no end; and much study is a weariness of the flesh" (Eccl. 12:12). On a sea of books that flood the marketplace, we launch this series of THRU THE BIBLE with the hope that it might draw many to the one Book, *The Bible.*

J. VERNON McGEE

ZEPHANIAH

The Book of
ZEPHANIAH

INTRODUCTION

Zephaniah identifies himself better than any of the other minor prophets. Habakkuk concealed himself in silence—we know nothing about his background—but Zephaniah goes to the opposite extreme and tells us more than is ordinary. He traces his lineage back to his great-great-grandfather, Hizkiah (whom we know as Hezekiah), king of Judah. In other words, Zephaniah was of the royal line.

Zephaniah located the time of his writing just as clearly as he did his identification: "in the days of Josiah the son of Amon, king of Judah" (Zeph. 1:1). It was a dark day for the nation. According to the arrangement of the Hebrew Scriptures, Zephaniah was the last of the prophets before the Captivity. He was contemporary with Jeremiah and perhaps with Micah, although I doubt that. His was the swan song of the Davidic kingdom, and he is credited with giving impetus to the revival during the reign of Josiah.

The little Book of Zephaniah will never take the place of John 3:16 and the Gospel of John as number one in Bible popularity. The contents of this book have never been familiar, and I doubt that it has been read very much. I dare say that few have ever heard a sermon on Zephaniah. One Sunday morning several years ago, as I was about to preach on this book, I asked the congregation how many had ever heard a message on Zephaniah before. Out of the 2500–3000 who were present, only two hands were raised! Such neglect is not due to the mediocrity or the inferiority of this little book. If its theme were known, I think it would be very much appreciated because it has the same theme as the Gospel of John. John is called the apostle of love; and as we study this book, we will find that Zephaniah is the prophet of love. That may be difficult for you to believe, but let me give you a verse to demonstrate my point. You are acquainted with John 3:16, but are you acquainted with Zephaniah 3:17?—"The LORD thy God in the midst of thee is mighty; he will save, he will rejoice over thee with joy; he will rest in his love, he will joy over thee with singing." This is lovely, is it not? However, Zephaniah is a little different from the Gospel of John, for this verse is just a small island which is sheltered in the midst of a storm-tossed sea. Much of this book seems rather harsh and cruel; it seems as if it is fury poured out. Chapter 3 opens in this vein: "Woe to her that is filthy and polluted, to the oppressing city!" (Zeph. 3:1). There is so much judgment in this little book; therefore, how can love be its theme? To find proof that love is the theme of this little books is like looking for the proverbial needle in a haystack, but I will illustrate my point by telling you a mystery story. This may seem to be a very peculiar way to begin a study of Zephaniah, but it is going to help us understand this little book. The title of my story is—

THE DARK SIDE OF LOVE

It was late at night in a suburban area of one of our great cities in America. A child lay restless in her bed. A man, with a very severe and stern look, stealthily entered her bedroom and softly approached her bed. The moment the little girl saw him, a terrified look came over her face, and she began to scream. Her mother rushed into the room and went over to her. The trembling child threw her arms about her mother.

The man withdrew to the telephone, called someone, who was evidently an accomplice, and in a very soft voice made some sort of an arrangement. Hastily the man reentered the room, tore the child from the mother's arms, and rushed out to a waiting car. The child was sobbing, and he attempted to stifle her cries. He drove madly down street after street until he finally pulled up before a large, sinister, and foreboding-looking building. All was quiet, the building was partially dark, but there was one room upstairs ablaze with light.

The child was hurriedly taken inside, up to the lighted room, and put into the hands of the man with whom the conversation had been held over the telephone in the hallway. In turn, the child was handed over to another accomplice—this time a woman—and these two took her into an inner room. The man who had brought her was left outside in the hallway. Inside the room, the man plunged a gleaming, sharp knife into the vitals of that little child, and she lay as if she were dead.

Your reaction at this point may be, "I certainly hope they will catch the criminal who abducted the little girl and is responsible for such an awful crime!"

However, I have not described to you the depraved and degraded action of a debased mind. I have not taken a chapter out of the life of the man in Cell 2455, Death Row. I have not related to you the sordid and sadistic crime of a psychopathic criminal. On the contrary, I have described to you a tender act of love. In fact, I can think of no more sincere demonstration of love than that which I have described to you. I am sure you are amazed when I say that. Let me fill in some of the details, and then you will understand.

You see, that little girl had awakened in the night with severe abdominal pain. She had been subject to such attacks before, and the doctor had told her parents to watch her very carefully. It was her father who had hurried into the room. When he saw the suffering of his little girl, he went to the telephone, called the family physician, and arranged to meet him at the hospital. He then rushed the little girl down to the hospital and handed her over to the family physician who took her to the operating room and performed emergency surgery.

Through it all, every move and every act of that father was of tender love, anxious care, and wise decision. I have described to you the dark side of love—but *love*, nevertheless. The father loved the child just as much on that dark night when he took her to the hospital and delivered her to the surgeon's knife as he did the next week when he brought her flowers and candy. It was just as much a demonstration of deep affection when he delivered her into the hands of the surgeon as it was the next week when he brought her home and delivered her into the arms of her mother. My friend, love places the eternal security and permanent welfare of the object of love above any transitory or temporary comfort or present pleasure down here upon this earth. Love seeks the best interests of the beloved. That is what this little Book of Zephaniah is all about—the dark side of love.

In our nation we have come through a period when the love of God has been exaggerated out of all proportion to the other attributes of our God. It has been presented on the sunny side of the street with nothing of the other side ever mentioned. There is a "love" of God presented that sounds to me like the doting of grandparents rather than the vital and vigorous concern of a parent for the best interests of the child.

The liberal preacher has chanted like a parrot. He has used shopworn clichés and tired adjectives. He has said, "God is love, God is love, God is love" until he has made it saccharin sweet; yet he has not told about the dark side of the love of God. He has watered down love, making it sickening rather than stimulating, causing it to slop over on every side like a sentimental feeling rather than an abiding concern for the object of love.

However, I want you to notice that there is the dark side of the love of God. He deals with us according to our needs, my friend. The Great Physician will put His child on the operating table. He will use the surgeon's knife when He sees a tumor of transgression or a deadly virus sapping our spiritual lives or the cancerous growth of sin. He does not hesitate to deal with us severely. We must learn this fact early: He loves us when He is subjecting us to surgery just as much as when He sends us candy and flowers and brings us into the sunshine.

Sometimes the Great Physician will operate without giving us so much as a sedative. But you can always be sure of one thing. When He does this, He will pour in the balm of Gilead. When He sees that it is best for you and for me to go down through the valley of suffering, that it will be for our eternal welfare, He will not hesitate to let us go down through that dark valley. Someone has expressed it in these lines:

> Is there no other way, Oh, God,
>   Except through sorrow, pain and loss,
> To stamp Christ's likeness on my soul,
>   No other way except the cross?

And then a voice stills all my soul,
 As stilled the waves of Galilee.
Can'st thou not bear the furnace,
 If midst the flames I walk with thee?

I bore the cross, I know its weight;
 I drank the cup I hold for thee.
Can'st thou not follow where I lead?
 I'll give thee strength, lean hard on Me!

My friend, He loves us most when He is operating on us, "For whom the Lord loveth he chasteneth . . ." (Heb. 12:6)—in other words, He child-trains, He disciplines us.

Under another figure, the Lord Jesus presented it yonder in the Upper Room to those who were His own. He said, in John 15:1–2: "I am the true vine, and my Father is the husbandman. Every branch in me that beareth not fruit he taketh away: and every branch that beareth fruit, he purgeth [prunes] it, that it may bring forth more fruit." We must remember that the Father reaches into your life and mine and prunes out that which is not fruitbearing—and it hurts! But, as a Puritan divine said years ago, "The husbandman is never so close to the branch as when he is trimming it." The Father is never more close to you, my friend, than when He is reaching in and taking out of your heart and life those things that offend.

It was Spurgeon who noticed a weather vane that a farmer had on his barn. It was an unusual weather vane, for on it the farmer had the words, GOD IS LOVE. Mr. Spurgeon asked him, "Do you mean by this that God's love is as changeable as the wind?" The farmer shook his head. "No," he said, "I do not mean that God's love changes like that. I mean that whichever way the wind blows, *God is love.*"

Today it may be the soft wind from the south that He brings to blow across your life, for He loves you. But tomorrow He may let the cold blasts from the north blow over your life—and if He does, He still loves you.

It has been expressed in these familiar lines in a way I never could express it myself:

God hath not promised skies always blue, ·
   Flower-strewn pathways all our lives through;
God hath not promised sun without rain,
   Joy without sorrow, peace without pain.

God hath not promised we shall not know
   Toil and temptation, trouble and woe;
He hath not told us we shall not bear
   Many a burden, many a care.

But God hath promised strength for the day,
   Rest for the laborer, light for the way,
Grace for the trials, help from above,
   Unfailing sympathy, undying love.
                    —Annie Johnson Flint

Beloved, if you are a child of God and are in a place of suffering, be assured and know that God loves you. Regardless of how it may appear, He loves you, and you cannot ever change that fact.

Sweetness and light are associated with love on every level and rightly so, but this aspect does not exhaust the full import of love. Love expresses itself always for the good of the one who is loved. This is the reason that it is difficult to associate love with the judgment of God. The popular notion of God is that He is a super Dr. Jekyll and Mr. Hyde. One nature of His is expressed by love, and the other nature is expressed by wrath in judgment. These two appear to be contrary to the extent that there seem to be two Gods. The Book of Zephaniah is filled with the wrath and judgment of God (see Zeph. 1:15; 3:8), but there is the undertone of the love of God (see Zeph. 3:17).

Let me now tell you a true story to illustrate the dark side of love. One Mother's Day, while I was still a pastor in downtown Los Angeles, I looked out over my congregation, and I could tell that there were many mothers present. They were dressed a little special for the day, and many of them were wearing corsages. But I also noticed one mother who did not look as happy as the others. There was a note of sorrow on her face, although she wore a beautiful orchid corsage, the biggest one I had ever seen. I knew that it came from her son in the

East. He is a prominent businessman, and high up in government circles as well, but he is not a Christian. He turns a deaf ear to his mother's pleadings. She prays for him constantly and asks others to pray for him. I recall that one Sunday morning she came to me, with tears streaming down her cheeks, and she said, "Oh, Dr. McGee, I pray that God will save my boy. I pray that He will save him even if he has to put him on a sickbed." Then, almost fiercely, she said, "Even if He has to *kill* him, I pray that God will save him before it is too late!" Suppose a detective from the police department had been listening to our conversation. Would he have arrested her for making that statement? No. He could not have arrested her at all. What she said was not a threat but was actually a statement of love. Because she loved that boy, she was actually willing to give him up and to let him go down through the doorway of death if it would mean the salvation of his soul.

The little prophecy of Zephaniah presents the dark side of the love of God. He is a God of love, but He is also a God of judgment. Zephaniah opens with the rumblings of judgment, and you will not find judgment enunciated in any more harsh manner than it is in this book.

Two thoughts stand out in this brief book:

1. "The day of the LORD" occurs seven times in this little prophecy. Obadiah and Joel, the first of the writing prophets, were the first to use this expression. All of the prophets refer to it; and now Zephaniah, the last of the writing prophets, before the Captivity, brings it to our attention again. He uses it more than any of the other prophets. The actual phrase occurs seven times, but there are other references to it. This expression has particular application to the Great Tribulation period, which precedes the Kingdom; but the Day of the Lord also includes the time of the Kingdom. The Great Tribulation period is ended by the coming of Christ personally to the earth to establish the millennial Kingdom—and all that is included in the Day of the Lord. The emphasis in the Book of Zephaniah is upon judgment. Joel also opens his prophecy with a description of a great locust plague, which he likens to the Day of the Lord that is coming in the future. Joel says that the Day of the Lord is not light; it is darkness. It is on the black

background of man's sin that God writes in letters of light the wonderful gospel story for you and me.

2. "Jealousy" occurs twice in this book. God's jealousy is on a little different plane from that of yours and mine. In our jealousy, we seek to do evil. God is jealous of those who are His own. He is jealous of mankind. He created him, and He has purchased a redemption for him, and made it possible for him to be saved. It is not His will that any should perish; He wants them saved—He is jealous for mankind. But when they don't turn to Him, He is going to judge them. The thing which the Book of Zephaniah makes clear is that God is glorified in judging as well as He is glorified in saving. A great many people cannot understand how that is possible. Ezekiel 38—39 speaks of the time in the future when God will judge Russia. We read there, "And thou shalt come up against my people of Israel, as a cloud to cover the land; it shall be in the latter days, and I will bring thee against my land, that the heathen may know me, when I shall be sanctified in thee, O Gog, before their eyes" (Ezek. 38:16). In other words, God is saying, "I intend to judge this godless nation, and when I do, I shall be glorified in that judgment." That is a tremendous statement for God to make, and for a great many people, it is a bitter pill to swallow. But it might be well for us to learn to think God's thoughts after Him, realizing that our thoughts are not His thoughts and our ways are not His ways at all.

OUTLINE

I. Judgment of Judah and Jerusalem, Chapter 1

II. Judgment of Earth and of All Nations, Chapters 2:1—3:8

III. All Judgments Removed; Kingdom Established, Chapter 3:9–20

CHAPTER 1

THEME: Judgment of Judah and Jerusalem

[handwritten: 19 KINGS IN BOTH ISRAEL & JUDAH / 31 YRS / THE BEST]

The word of the Lᴏʀᴅ which came unto Zephaniah the son of Cushi, the son of Gedaliah, the son of Amariah, the son of Hizkiah, in the days of Josiah the son of Amon, king of Judah [Zeph. 1:1].

[handwritten: SOUTH]

Zephaniah identifies himself as being of the royal family. Hezekiah, king of Judah, was his great-great-grandfather. Zephaniah prophesied during the days of the reign of Josiah, which was the period of the last spiritual movement that took place in the southern kingdom of Judah. There was a revival during that time—it wasn't a great one, it didn't last long, but there was a revival. Zephaniah knew something of the reigns of Amon, an evil king, and of Manasseh, also a terrible king. He saw that judgment was coming upon his nation and upon his people, and his message is a very harsh one.

[handwritten: 606 BC / 55 YRS]

I will utterly consume all things from off the land, saith the Lᴏʀᴅ [Zeph. 1:2].

This is certainly strong language. God says, "I intend to judge, and when I do, I will actually scrape the land. The land will be as if a dirt scraper had been run over it. Just as you wipe clean a dish, that is the way I intend to judge them."

As we move further into this prophecy, we will recognize that this judgment covers more than just the land of Israel. It is a worldwide devastation that is predicted here. The Book of Revelation confirms this and places the time of this judgment as the Great Tribulation period. During that period, this earth will absolutely be denuded by the judgments that will come upon it. This will occur right before God brings in the millennial Kingdom and renews the earth.

[handwritten: 2ND ½ OF 7 YRS / STRIPPED]

**I will consume man and beast; I will consume the fowls
of the heaven, and the fishes of the sea, and the
stumblingblocks with the wicked; and I will cut off man
from the land, saith the LORD [Zeph. 1:3].**

"I will consume man and beast"—all living creatures are included in
this judgment. When I was in the land of Israel, I was told that they
have a zoo somewhere up around the Sea of Galilee. They are making
an effort to gather together the animals that were in existence in Bible
days and to put them in this zoo. Obviously, as the population of Israel
increases, the same thing will happen as has happened in the United
States. Certain animal species will become extinct and disappear.
God says that this is exactly what is going to happen when He judges
that land. Many species—in fact, all of them—will become extinct at
that time. This is to be a very severe judgment.

SOUTHERN

JOSHA
10:5
PAGAN
PRIEST

**I will also stretch out mine hand upon Judah, and upon
all the inhabitants of Jerusalem; and I will cut off the
remnant of Baal from this place, and the name of the
Chemarims with the priests [Zeph. 1:4].**

2 KING 23:5

"I will also stretch out mine hand upon Judah, and upon all the inhabitants of Jerusalem." God now makes it clear that Judah and Jerusalem are to be singled out for judgment.

"I will cut off the remnant of Baal from this place." The thing that
brings the judgment of God upon the land is very specific"—it is idolatry. In the prophecy of Habakkuk, God mentions five woes He was
going to bring upon the people because of certain sins which they had
committed. Idolatry was the last one; it was the fifth woe. But here
Zephaniah narrows it down and puts his hand on idolatry—that is,
false religion.

The Scriptures, beginning with the Book of Judges, teach a philosophy of human government, which you will find was true of God's
people and which has been true of every nation. The first step in a
nation's decline is *religious apostasy,* a turning from the living and

1ST COMMANDMENT - MOST IMPORTANT

true God. The second step downward for a nation is _moral awfulness._
The third step downward is _political anarchy_.

A great many people in the United States today think that our problem is in Washington, D.C.—I don't think so. Another group of people feel that if people could be reformed, if we could get people to act nicely, not be violent and not steal, if we could just lift our moral standards, then that would solve our problems. Again, I don't think that is the problem. Very frankly, I believe that the problem in this country is religious apostasy. The problem is out yonder with you and right here with me. The problem is that the church has failed to give God's message. I am not talking about _every_ church or _your_ church necessarily. There are many Bible-teaching churches across this country which have wonderful pastors who are standing for God—and I thank God for them. But the great denominations, by and large, have now departed from the faith. They have come to the place where they no longer give an effective message to the nation. As a result, from this religious apostasy have flowed moral awfulness and political anarchy.

If you think that this is just the wild raving of a fundamentalist preacher, you are wrong. Let me quote an excerpt from an editorial in a major metropolitan newspaper a number of years ago. Speaking of the failure of the churches to present any spiritual message whatsoever, the editorial concluded:

> This betrayal of Christ in the name of Christianity is one reason for the moral and spiritual malaise with which this country is afflicted. The melancholy fact is that the churches no longer influence the development of national character. People go to church mainly because of an impulse to participate in a service of worship, not because of any spiritual guidance they expect from the clergyman.

What a note of condemnation this is! This is true not just of our nation but of every nation.

The historian Gibbon concluded that there were five reasons for the decline and fall of Rome. Gibbon was not a Christian, but here is why he says Rome fell: (1) The undermining of the dignity and sanctity of the home, which is the basis of human society. (2) Higher and higher taxes; the spending of public money for free bread and circuses for the populace. (3) The mad craze for pleasure; sports becoming every year more exciting, more brutal, more immoral. (4) The building of great armaments when the great enemy was within; the decay of individual responsibility. (5) The decay of religion, fading into mere form, losing touch with life, losing power to guide the people.

The message of Zephaniah carries out this scriptural principle of human government, and he puts his finger right down on the sore spot in the southern kingdom of Judah—idolatry. Zephaniah saw what was happening. The people were now on the toboggan; they were on the way down and out, and judgment was coming. Idolatry is where every great nation has gone off the track. When a nation departs from the living and true God or when it gives up great moral principles which were based on religion, when it goes into idolatry, these factors eventually lead it into gross immorality and into political anarchy.

The interesting thing is that three kinds of idolatry, I believe, are mentioned to us here. "I will cut off the remnant of Baal from this place." The first form of idolatry is the worship of Baal which was introduced into the northern kingdom by Jezebel whose father was the high priest of the worship among the Sidonians. In the southern kingdom, the worship of Baal was popularized and the altars of Baal were rebuilt during the reign of Manasseh. This is an instance which illustrates why it would be wonderful to study at the same time the corresponding portions of the prophetic and historical books of Scripture. At this point it would be helpful to read the background of the reign of Manasseh (see 2 Kings 21; 2 Chron. 33). No king ever departed as far from God as this man did. He reintroduced the worship of Baal, which was a very immoral form of worship. Along with the worship of Baal was worship of Ashtoreth. When the female principal is introduced in deity, you have gross immorality; and that, of course, came into the life of the nation during this period. Baal worship was a form, therefore, of nature worship and was very crude indeed. When Josiah

Jud 2:11-23

became king (he was a good king), the first thing he did was to try to remove the worship of Baal.

"And the name of the Chemarims with the priests." *Chemarims* actually means "black priests"—they wore black garments. Have you noticed that those who engage in the worship of Satan today don black garments? It is quite interesting that it is not original with them. It comes all the way down from these idolatrous priests who wore black robes. Zephaniah says that these priests are to be judged.

And them that worship the host of heaven upon the housetops; and them that worship and that swear by the Lord, and that swear by Malcham [Zeph. 1:5].

"And them that worship the host of heaven upon the housetops." Zephaniah now mentions the second form of idolatry that became prevalent in that land. It was more subtle and very dangerous indeed. Their housetops were flat—that is true even today in the land of Israel. It is the place where the family gathered in the evening. In fact, God gave a law about putting a banister, a railing, around the roof so that no one would fall off. Zephaniah says that the housetop became a place of worship, and you can see how idolatry was moving into the homes. It meant that actually every home was a little heathen temple where idolatry was practiced; idolatry was really reaching into the homes.

"Them that worship the host of heaven"—the sun, the moon, the stars. It was a worship of the creature rather than the Creator. They worshiped that which had been made rather than worshiping the Creator. This was the second form of idolatry which they adopted.

The worst, the most sophisticated, and the most subtle of all the forms of idolatry, is the one that is mentioned next—"and them that worship and that swear by the Lord, and that swear by Malcham." Malcham is the name of Molech, the god of the Ammonites. It was a worship in which they actually sacrificed their children. The subtlety of it was that at the same time they professed to worship the living and true God. They went to the temple. They said that they knew the Lord, that they believed in God. But they also worshiped Molech—they were doing both.

This is the subtle thing that is also taking place today. There are many so-called churches that by the wildest stretch of the imagination could never be called Christian churches. The true church is built around a person, and that person is Jesus Christ. The early church met together to worship and adore *Him*, to come to know Him, and to have fellowship around Him. Everything they did pointed to Jesus Christ. How many churches do you know of where Christ is not even mentioned? If He is mentioned, He is mentioned in a derogatory manner. In other words, His deity is denied. They deny that He is God. They do not worship Him, but they give lip service to Him. They talk about the teachings of Jesus and about what a wonderful man He was. They even call Him a "superstar"! But they deny everything that has been set down in the Scriptures for us as Christians. It is a castrated Christianity that is abroad today.

This is the kind of subtle idolatry that was coming up in the land of Judah in that day. People were still going through the rituals, still going to the temple on the Sabbath. I don't think they came any other time, but they were there then. However, they were actually worshiping Molech. Molech was the god of the flesh. It was a fleshly worship—again, there was gross immorality. Likewise today, there are those who go to church—they have a churchianity but not a Christianity. They deny the great facts of the Christian faith. They practice immorality, or they practice things that are contrary to the Word of God. This is the picture of Judah in that day, and it is the subtlety of the hour in which we live. A great many people think that if a building has a steeple on it, a bell in that steeple, an organ, a big center aisle for weddings, a pulpit down front, and a choir loft, these make it a church. My friend, it may be one of the worst spots in town! It may be worse than any barroom, any gambling establishment, or any brothel in town. This is the thing that is so deceptive. The thing that undermined the nation of Judah is that they *pretended* that they were serving the living and true God, but they were giving themselves over to Molech idolatry.

> **And them that are turned back from the LORD; and those that have not sought the LORD, nor inquired for him [Zeph. 1:6].**

The people have turned completely from God. Two classes are mentioned: backsliders and those who were never saved.

> **Hold thy peace at the presence of the Lord GOD: for the day of the LORD is at hand: for the LORD hath prepared a sacrifice, he hath bid his guests [Zeph. 1:7].**

"Hold thy peace at the presence of the Lord GOD." The suggestion is, "Hush, hush. Don't talk out. Don't speak out. No protesting. You are in the presence of the living God." There is a great lack of reverence for God today. This notion that Jesus is sort of a buddy, that God is the man upstairs, and that we can be very flippant when we speak of Him, is all wrong. May I say to you, our God is a holy God. If you and I were to come within a billion miles of Him, we would fall down on our faces before Him because of who He is. He is the great God, the Creator of the universe, and we are merely little creatures.

"Hold thy peace at the presence of the Lord GOD." Why? "For the day of the LORD is at hand." This is the first mention of the Day of the Lord in this book. The Day of the Lord is presented here primarily as the time of judgment. If you want to fit it into God's program, it is the Great Tribulation period—that is when it begins. Today, you and I are living in the day of Christ, the day of grace. The Day of the Lord will begin when the church leaves this earth. Then God will begin to move in judgment.

Prior to that day, which is still in the future, there have been times which have been likened unto the Day of the Lord. When Nebuchadnezzar finally came and destroyed Jerusalem, burned it to the ground, and plowed it under, he left that land denuded. If you go to that land today, there are very few trees. Oh, I know that Israel has planted millions of trees, but you see barren hills everywhere. At one time those hills were all covered with trees and vineyards. It was a land of milk and honey, but it is not that today. There is still evidence of that which the enemy did. The Babylonians who came under Nebuchadnezzar were followed later by the Medo-Persians, then Alexander the Great, and finally the Romans. Enemy after enemy has come into that land. As a result, very few trees are left, and the land is almost completely denuded today. God made it very clear that that was what He was going to do—and He did it. The evidence is still there today. That judgment was for those people "the day of the LORD," but it does not completely satisfy these prophecies. Zephaniah makes it very clear that the Day of the Lord is that day which is yet in the future and which will be consummated when Christ comes and establishes His Kingdom here upon this earth.

With almost biting sarcasm, Zephaniah says, "For the LORD hath prepared a sacrifice, he hath bid his guests." The guests are going to be the sacrifice, by the way, and the sacrifice is the judgment that is coming upon this nation.

> **And it shall come to pass in the day of the LORD'S sacrifice, that I will punish the princes, and the king's children, and all such as are clothed with strange apparel [Zeph. 1:8].**

The thought here is that the rulers had turned away from God. All you have to do is to refer to the time when Zedekiah reigned. He was the last of the kings, and he actually saw his own children killed right before his eyes, and then his own eyes were put out (see 2 Kings 24—25). That was surely harsh judgment, but they had had the warning from God. To these people, this was like the Day of the Lord.

> **In the same day also will I punish all those that leap on the threshold, which fill their masters' houses with violence and deceit [Zeph. 1:9].**

Dr. Charles Feinberg (*Habakkuk, Zephaniah, Haggai, and Malachi,* p. 48) writes, "What is referred to is the zeal with which the servants of the rich hastened from their homes to plunder the property of others to enrich their masters." There were those who would take over the land and the homes of the poor. What was happening in that day was that the great middle class disappeared and you had the extreme rich and the extreme poor. The same thing is certainly happening in my own country today. God says to these people that He is going to judge them for this.

> **And it shall come to pass in that day, saith the LORD, that there shall be the noise of a cry from the fish gate, and an howling from the second, and a great crashing from the hills [Zeph. 1:10].**

"And it shall come to pass in that day"—this is clearly a reference to the Day of the Lord.

"That there shall be the noise of a cry from the fish gate." The fish gate is what is known today as the Damascus Gate. It was the gate through which they brought the fish from the Sea of Galilee and the Jordan River. It is located on the north side of the city of Jerusalem.

"And an howling from the second, and a great crashing from the hills." The Damascus Gate today is down in a rather low place. If you are acquainted with Jerusalem, you know that the city is surrounded by hills. Zephaniah is saying that in any direction you would want to move, there will be this wailing of the people when the time of judgment has come upon them.

> **Howl, ye inhabitants of Maktesh, for all the merchant people are cut down; all they that bear silver are cut off [Zeph. 1:11].**

Maktesh means "mortar." There is supposed to have been a depression in the city of Jerusalem where the marketplace was situated. It was perhaps the cheesemakers' valley. It was the valley that went alongside the temple where the Wailing Wall is today—which is a good place for it. "Howl, ye inhabitants of Maktesh, for all the merchant people are cut down; all they that bear silver are cut off."

And it shall come to pass at that time, that I will search Jerusalem with candles, and punish the men that are settled on their lees: that say in their heart, The LORD will not do good, neither will he do evil [Zeph. 1:12].

"And it shall come to pass at that time, that I will search Jerusalem with candles." In other words, it is like taking a flashlight and going to look for an individual who is hiding in the dark. God says, "I intend to search out Jerusalem just like that. I will bring to light all the evil and the sin."

"And punish the men that are settled on their lees." This is an idiomatic expression that corresponds, I think, to our idiom today when we say, "Take it easy." These people were taking it easy. They did not believe they would be judged any more than people today believe that we are to be judged as a nation.

"That say in their heart, The LORD will not do good, neither will he do evil." They are saying, "God's doing nothing. God is not going to do anything about it." Habakkuk's question was, "Why don't you do something about the evil, Lord?" God told him, "I *am* doing something." And when Habakkuk was given a vision and saw what God was really doing, he cried out to God for mercy for the people. A great many people today say, "I'll ignore God. He doesn't do good. He doesn't do evil." They are absolutely neutral about God. This type of thinking, of course, is what led to the abominable theology that God is dead. Only a society like ours could have produced that kind of theology, because people in an affluent society say, "We don't need God at all." As a result, they think that He doesn't do good, He doesn't do evil, He doesn't do anything. But they are greatly mistaken, and Zephaniah is going to make that very clear to us.

Therefore their goods shall become a booty, and their houses a desolation: they shall also build houses, but not inhabit them; and they shall plant vineyards, but not drink the wine thereof [Zeph. 1:13].

"Therefore their goods shall become a booty." The goods which they took by plundering and pillaging and robbing are going to be taken away from them in just the same way as they got them.

"And their houses a desolation"—in other words, there would be ghost towns in Israel.

"They shall also build houses, but not inhabit them; and they shall plant vineyards, but not drink the wine thereof." God had given a law to these people that when a man planted a vineyard, he was not to go to war until he had eaten the fruit of that vineyard. Another law said that if a man married, he was to be excused from going to war for a year. Here God is saying that they are going to plant vineyards, but they are not going to drink the wine of them because they have sinned. They won't be able to take time off from warfare. Neither will they be able to take time off when they get married because the enemy is going to come in like a flood.

The great day of the Lord is near, it is near, and hasteth greatly, even the voice of the day of the Lord: the mighty man shall cry there bitterly [Zeph. 1:14].

"The great day of the Lord is near." This great Day of the Lord is the time of the Great Tribulation in the future. In Zephaniah's day, after Josiah ruled, there never arose in the southern kingdom another good king. Every one of them was bad. Jehoahaz, Jehoiakim, Jehoiachin, Zedekiah—every one of them was a corrupt king. Now judgment is going to come upon the nation and upon the people for their departure from God. But they are going to experience only a very small portion of what is in the future in the great Day of the Lord.

Zephaniah says, "It is near, and hasteth greatly, even the voice of the day of the Lord: the mighty man shall cry there bitterly." In other words, the concept of the Wailing Wall would come into existence. And it is going to be there until after the Great Tribulation period because Israel will never know peace until the Prince of Peace comes and they acknowledge their Messiah.

> That day is a day of wrath, a day of trouble and distress,
> a day of wasteness and desolation, a day of darkness
> and gloominess, a day of clouds and thick darkness
> [Zeph. 1:15].

Dr. Charles Feinberg is an excellent Hebrew scholar, and he calls our attention to many things that you and I would normally pass over. I would highly recommend to you his work on the minor prophets. There is a play upon words in this verse that Dr. Feinberg brings out which we miss in the English, of course: "The Hebrew words for wasteness and desolation—sho'ah and umesho'ah—are alike in sound to convey the monotony of the destruction." But we do have in the English an alliteration that reveals something of it. It is a day of trouble, then distress, desolation, darkness, and thick darkness, so that there is a play upon words even in the English.

Zephaniah is speaking here of the harshness, the intensity of the judgment that is coming, and the question naturally arises: How can a God of love do a thing like this? We will find before we finish our study of this book that it is like the story I told in the Introduction of the father who took his little child to the surgeon to be operated upon. The picture can be presented in such a way that it looks like he is being cruel and harsh to bring her to the doctor who will plunge his knife into her. But actually, everything the father did was out of love for his little girl. Even the great day of wrath is a judgment of God, but it has in it the love of God. Regardless of what takes place, God is love. It is like the farmer who had on his barn the weather vane which said on it, GOD IS LOVE. The farmer explained it by saying, "Regardless of which way the wind blows, God is love." That is true, my friend.

Even in judgment, God is still a God of love. And He judges because it is essential for Him to judge that which is evil. He does that because He has to be true to Himself, and He could not be good to His creatures unless He did that. If God is going to permit sin throughout eternity, if God does not intend to judge sin, if you and I are going to have to wrestle with disease and with heartbreak and with disappointment and with sorrow throughout eternity, I cannot conceive that He is a God of love. But if you tell me that God is going to judge sin, that He is coming in with a mighty judgment, and that He is going to remove sin from His universe, I'm going to say, "Hallelujah!" And I will believe that He is a God of love even when He does that.

A day of the trumpet and alarm against the fenced cities, and against the high towers [Zeph. 1:16].

When God gave to the nation Israel the trumpets that they were to blow on the wilderness march, there were several ways in which they were to be used. Having mentioned the different ways the two silver trumpets were to be used, the Lord says in Numbers 10:9, "And if ye go to war in your land against the enemy that oppresseth you, then ye shall blow an alarm with the trumpets; and ye shall be remembered before the LORD your God, and ye shall be saved from your enemies." Zephaniah says here that it is "a day of the trumpet"; they are going to blow the alarm, but God does not intend to deliver them. Why? He intended to judge them. He intends to deliver them over to the enemy, not deliver them from the enemy. It is to be "A day of the trumpet and alarm against the fenced cities, and against the high towers."

CITY STATES

And I will bring distress upon men, that they shall walk like blind men, because they have sinned against the LORD: and their blood shall be poured out as dust, and their flesh as the dung [Zeph. 1:17].

This is extreme judgment, I'll grant you. But, you know, surgery today is extreme. After my doctor operated on me the first time for cancer, I was asking him about the operation. He told me, "I cut on you until there was almost a question as to which pile was McGee!" It's a pretty harsh thing to cut on a fellow like that, but my doctor didn't do it because he was angry with me. He didn't do it even in judgment. He did it actually to save my life, and I believe that on the human level he did save my life by that severe method. May I say to you, God will judge, and He does it in an extreme way. He does extreme surgery, but He does it for the sake of the body politic.

> Neither their silver nor their gold shall be able to deliver them in the day of the Lord's wrath; but the whole land shall be devoured by the fire of his jealousy: for he shall make even a speedy riddance of all them that dwell in the land [Zeph. 1:18].

It has been quite interesting that this nation in which I live has spent billions of dollars throughout the world trying to buy friends, trying to win friends and influence people. But we are hated throughout the world today—we are not loved. You cannot buy love; you cannot win people over with silver and gold. But in this country we still believe that money solves all the ills of this life, that money is the answer to all the problems. God says that when He begins to judge, "neither their silver nor their gold shall be able to deliver them in the day of the Lord's wrath."

"But the whole land shall be devoured by the fire of his jealousy: for he shall make even a speedy riddance of all them that dwell in the land." God removed them from the land. Why did He do that? He did that because He loved them. If He had not done it, it would have been necessary to exterminate totally succeeding generations. For the sake of the future generations—so not all would have to be slain—God had to move in and cut away the cancer of sin that was destroying the nation.

CHAPTER 2

THEME: Judgment of the earth and of all nations

God has not only judged His own people, but God also judges the nations; and that is the subject of this chapter and through verse 8 of chapter 3. But God is gracious, long-suffering, and not willing that any should perish; therefore, He sends out a final call. Although you would think that He had reached the end of His patience, in the first three verses we find Zephaniah sending out God's last call to the nation of Judah to repent and to come to Him.

> **Gather yourselves together, yea, gather together, O nation not desired [Zeph. 2:1].**

"Gather yourselves together." They are to come together as a people, as Dr. Feinberg has stated it, ". . . to a religious assembly to entreat the favor of the Lord in order that by prayer He may turn away His judgment" (*Habakkuk, Zephaniah, Haggai, and Malachi*, p. 53).

"Yea, gather together, O nation not desired." Their sin, of course, has caused God to bring judgment upon them. But it is not that He does not desire them; it is not because He does not love them. Judgment came upon them because of their sin. They were repugnant, they were repulsive; yet they were insensible to the shame of their sinful condition. Their sin had reached a very low stage, and they were dead to shame; they had no sense of decency at all. They were shameless in their conduct. We would say that they had no sensitivity to sin whatsoever. They sinned with impudence. They would sin openly and actually boast of it.

We have come to that same place as a nation today. Someone said to me not long ago, "Dr. McGee, you speak as if America is sinning more and is in a worse condition today than it ever was before." I do not mean to imply that at all. However, I do not believe that there was just as much sin when I was growing up as there is today, but the sin was carried on behind the curtain or in the backyard or someplace else where it could not be seen. It was not flaunted before the world. It was not boasted of. In other words, it was not shameless sin as it is at the present time. I heard a very beautiful young woman on a talk program on television boast of the fact that she is living with a man to whom she is not married. The others on the program congratulated her for her "courage" and "broad-mindedness." Nobody called it shameless sin. Sin is right out in the open today. I don't think there is more sin— it is just out in the open where you can see it. They sinned in my day, that's for sure, but it was done under cover. It was done secretly, and there was a sense of sorrow for sin which we seem to have lost today. You and I do not know how repulsive our sin is to God. We spend very little time weeping over our sins.

> Before the decree bring forth, before the day pass as the chaff, before the fierce anger of the Lord come upon you, before the day of the Lord's anger come upon you [Zeph. 2:2].

God says, "Come together for prayer. Come together for repentance. Come together and turn to Me." There is a note of urgency here. Zephaniah is saying to the people, "Do this before God begins to move in judgment, because when you pass over the line and God begins to move in judgment, you will find out it's too late."

One of the things that is needed today in my country is for someone whose voice is heard to call our nation to prayer and to repentance. My nation has almost reached the end of its rope. This is a great need, and that kind of prayer God will hear and answer.

> Seek ye the Lord, all ye meek of the earth, which have wrought his judgment; seek righteousness, seek meekness: it may be ye shall be hid in the day of the Lord's anger [Zeph. 2:3].

"Seek ye the Lord, all ye meek of the earth, which have wrought his judgment." There has always been a remnant of those people who are true to God just as there is a remnant in the church today. I doubt that there are many churches—no matter how liberal they may be—who are without some members who are real believers. Now I don't understand why they are there, and I don't propose to sit in judgment on them, but there is a remnant within the liberal church today. God has always had a remnant in the world, and apparently He is speaking here to those who are the godly remnant in Judah.

"Seek righteousness." The remnant also should be very careful of the way they live their lives. "Seek meekness." They are not to be lifted up by arrogance and pride and self-sufficiency, for that was one of the great sins of the nation. This is also a danger among believers today. Someone has said that there is "a pride of race, a pride of face, and a pride of grace." Some people are even proud that they have been saved by grace! They feel that that is something for them to boast about. They feel that they are the peculiar and particular pets of almighty God because of their salvation! My friend, we have nothing to glory in. The apostle Paul said that he had nothing to glory in, and believe me, if Paul didn't have anything to glory in, I'm sure that none of us has. There is a danger of being proud of the fact that we are God's children, but it ought rather to lead to meekness. He says here, "Seek righteousness, seek meekness."

"It may be ye shall be hid in the day of the Lord's anger." It is a glorious, wonderful thing to be hidden in the cleft of the rock and to be covered by His wings. God's children need to recognize that, although they will not go through the Great Tribulation period, they may experience a great deal of judgment and a great deal of trouble just as these people did. Judah did not go through the Great Tribulation, the great Day of the Lord, but they certainly were going through, as I like to put it, "the little tribulation period." All of us are going to have tribulation to a certain extent in this life—we are going to have trouble. I heard the story years ago of a woman who was a maid and was complaining about her troubles. Apparently she had quite a few of them. When the lady of the house rather rebuked her for complaining, the woman replied, "When the good Lord sends me tribulation, I intend to tribulate." I agree with her. I believe we ought to tribulate. Paul says that we groan within these bodies, but that does not mean we are in the Great Tribulation nor that there is a chance of our going through it.

We come now to a section, beginning with verse 4 and going on down to verse 8 of chapter 3, in which we see the judgment of the nations. This passage reveals that God judges *all* the nations of this earth. The God of the Bible is not a local deity. He is not one that you put on a shelf. He is not one that is local or national. It has been the great error of the white race when attempting to "Christianize" a people by bringing them the gospel, also to try to make them live as we live and to adopt our customs and our methods. Well, there are a lot of different people on the topside of this earth, and they are all people for whom Christ died. Our business is to get them to hear the gospel, to get the Word of God to them, and then let *them* work their Christian life into their own customs and into their own patterns of life. I am told that my ancestors in Europe were pagan, eating raw meat, and living in caves, and when the gospel was brought to them, it did a great deal for them. The early missionaries who came to my ancestors didn't try to make them like they were. Apparently, the missionaries let them develop their own civilization, and we should do the same thing with others.

The God of the Bible is the God of this universe. He is the Creator of the universe and of mankind. Notice that He is going to judge these other nations, not just His own people. And He judges other nations for their *sin*. God has put up certain standards that have become worldwide. They have been written into the Ten Commandments, which God gave to Moses. All nations have a sense of right and wrong, although they may vary on what is right and what is wrong. A missionary was telling me about a tribe he had worked with out in the South Seas. They were headhunters; they were cannibals. But he said that they had a high sense of honesty. He told me that you could take your pocketbook with your money in it and put it down in the center of where the tribe dwelt and leave it there for a week, and nobody would touch it. But, of course, they didn't mind eating their mother-in-law for dinner. (You would never know exactly what they meant when they said they had their mother-in-law over for dinner—whether she came over to eat with them or whether they ate *her!*) But they did have a high sense of honesty, which is something I don't think we have in my country today. A lady told me that she left her purse on the counter in a department store, and when she returned in less than a minute, the purse was gone with no trace of it anywhere. But, of course, that thief was not going to eat his mother-in-law for dinner that evening. Standards apparently vary, but God has given to the nations of the world certain standards. You find them in all the nations of the earth. No nation could be a civilized nation if it did not recognize some of these. But when a people depart from the living and true God, they go into the deepest kind of paganism and heathenism and reach a place where God gives them up.

God now begins His judgment of the nations—

For Gaza shall be forsaken, and Ashkelon a desolation: they shall drive out Ashdod at the noon day, and Ekron shall be rooted up [Zeph. 2:4].

Mentioned here are four of the cities of the Philistines which are going to be judged. Somebody might ask, "Why didn't He mention Gath? It was a prominent place." Well, at this time Gath was pretty much under the control of the southern kingdom of Judah. These four cities are to be judged—Gaza, Ashkelon, Ashdod, and Ekron.

"For Gaza shall be forsaken, and Ashkelon a desolation." It is interesting that Gaza is forsaken today, and Ashkelon is a desolation. There is a place called Ashkelon, but it is not over the ruins of the old city. The old one is right down by the sea. I have been there and have seen the ruins of the temple of Dagon that are there.

"They shall drive out Ashdod at the noon day." Ashdod was driven out, and it was done at noonday. In that land, the people always take time off at noontime; that is, they have what is called south of the border a siesta. In some places in South America, you cannot get into a store from around twelve to two o'clock in the afternoon. You are just wasting your time if you try to go shopping because nothing will be open. You can get into a store at nine o'clock at night, but they take time for a siesta in the heat of the day. At Ashdod it's pretty warm. Although it is by the sea, it gets very warm there in the summer.

700 B.C. Time Frame

Zephaniah says that it will be destroyed and that they will be driven out at noonday. In other words, the enemy will take them off guard. Ashdod was completely obliterated. Israel possesses that territory today. They have built apartment building after apartment building, an oil refinery, and also a port there. It is one of the principal ports now. But in that day it was absolutely cleaned off. There are no ruins there at all.

"And Ekron shall be rooted up." Ekron was rooted up; it was completely removed.

Ez 25:16
1 Sam 30:14
2 Sm 8:18

Woe unto the inhabitants of the sea coast, the nation of the Cherethites! the word of the Lord is against you; O Canaan, the land of the Philistines, I will even destroy thee, that there shall be no inhabitant [Zeph. 2:5].

"Woe unto the inhabitants of the sea coast." All these places are along the seacoast.

"The nation of the Cherethites!" The Cherethites were people who came from the island of Crete, and they evidently were the Philistines. The word Philistine comes from the Hebrew word for migration. They immigrated to that country. This, by the way, ought to answer the question that some people, especially the liberals, have raised: "What right did Israel have to drive the Philistines out of their native land?" It was not their native land. Actually, Israel was there long before the Philistines were there. Abraham, Isaac, and Jacob, and their offspring were in that land, and then they went down to the land of Egypt. In that interval, the Philistines came into that country.

"The word of the Lord is against you; O Canaan, the land of the Philistines, I will even destroy thee, that there shall be no inhabitant." He says that they are to be judged. By the way, when was the last time you saw a Philistine? They have disappeared.

And the sea coast shall be dwellings and cottages for shepherds, and folds for flocks [Zeph. 2:6].

This took place, and this condition existed for over a thousand years—in fact, almost nineteen hundred years.

> And the coast shall be for the remnant of the house of
> Judah; they shall feed thereupon: in the houses of
> Ashkelon shall they lie down in the evening: for the
> Lord their God shall visit them, and turn away their
> captivity [Zeph. 2:7].

This is God's promise to His people that He will return them from their captivity to inhabit the land of Philistia, which was a part of the territory God had given to Abraham. I have pictures of Israelis lying on the beach at Ashkelon during a holiday. It is a beautiful, sandy beach on the Mediterranean Sea. This prophecy is a picture of a scene that can be demonstrated any day of the year, although it may change tomorrow. However, I do not consider what we see there today as a fulfillment of prophecy, because I believe that Israel will be driven from that land again before their final return under God.

Now He moves over from the west to the east and to the nations which were contiguous to the land of Judah—

> I have heard the reproach of Moab, and the revilings of
> the children of Ammon, whereby they have reproached
> my people, and magnified themselves against their bor-
> der.
>
> Therefore as I live, saith the Lord of hosts, the God of
> Israel, Surely Moab shall be as Sodom, and the children
> of Ammon as Gomorrah, even the breeding of nettles,
> and saltpits, and a perpetual desolation: the residue of
> my people shall spoil them, and the remnant of my peo-
> ple shall possess them [Zeph. 2:8-9].

I have visited a few countries in my lifetime, and the poorest country that I have ever been in is the modern nation of the Hashimite Kingdom of Jordan. It occupies what was the land of the Moabites and the Ammonites. The modern capital there is Amman. You just do not find any more desolate country than that. All of this prophecy has been fulfilled in the past.

Assyria

> This shall they have for their pride, because they have
> reproached and magnified themselves against the peo-
> ple of the Lord of hosts [Zeph. 2:10].

They are judged for their pride, and as you know, pride is the way the
devil sinned at the beginning.

> The Lord will be terrible unto them: for he will famish
> all the gods of the earth; and men shall worship him,
> every one from his place, even all the isles of the heathen
> [Zeph. 2:11].

God is going to judge the nations of the world because they have ig-
nored Him. They have not recognized Him. ". . . when they knew
God, they glorified him not as God, neither were thankful; but became
vain in their imaginations, and their foolish heart was darkened. Pro-
fessing themselves to be wise, they became fools; And changed the
glory of the uncorruptible God into an image made like to corruptible
man, and to birds, and fourfooted beasts, and creeping things" (Rom.
1:21–23). This is the reason God will judge them.

> Ye Ethiopians also, ye shall be slain by my sword [Zeph.
> 2:12].

Ethiopia is in Africa. You see, this is a *worldwide* judgment.

> And he will stretch out his hand against the north, and
> destroy Assyria; and will make Nineveh a desolation,
> and dry like a wilderness [Zeph. 2:13].

"And he will stretch out his hand against the north, and destroy Assyria." Ethiopia is in the south, but now we move to the north and find
that Assyria also is to be judged. In Zephaniah's day, Assyria was
making quite a splash in the world.

"And will make Nineveh a desolation, and dry like a wilderness."

That is the way Nineveh is today. The modern city of Mosul is across the Tigris River from the site of old Nineveh, and it is a miserable place, so I'm told. Nineveh and all of that area is still a desolation.

> And flocks shall lie down in the midst of her, all the beasts of the nations: both the cormorant and the bittern shall lodge in the upper lintels of it; their voice shall sing in the windows; desolation shall be in the thresholds: for he shall uncover the cedar work [Zeph. 2:14].

Birds study person

In other words, their buildings are to be torn down.

> This is the rejoicing city that dwelt carelessly, that said in her heart, I am, and there is none beside me: how is she become a desolation, a place for beasts to lie down in! every one that passeth by her shall hiss, and wag his hand [Zeph. 2:15].

"Every one that passeth by her shall hiss." People will hiss at Nineveh in the sense that it will be sort of an explosive expletive that comes from a person who is surprised: "Why, I thought that Assyria was a great nation and that Nineveh was a great city! Just look at it in desolation and ruin!" They hiss, and their breath is just blown out of them, as it were.

"And wag his hand." They will simply shake their hands back and forth, being absolutely stupefied to see what has taken place through God's judgment of the nations.

God has judged nations in the past, and God judges nations today. The Lord Jesus says that He will judge nations in the future. As we see in the Book of Habakkuk, God was moving in that day in a way that the prophet never suspected. And, my friend, God is moving in the nations of the world today. He has judged them in the past. He will judge them in the future.

CHAPTER 3

THEME: *Judgment of the earth and of all nations; all judgments removed and the Kingdom established*

The first eight verses of this chapter conclude this section, which deals with the judgment of the earth and of all nations. By now you may be tired of listening to Zephaniah talk about the harsh, the extreme, the unmitigating judgment of God upon His people. This is probably the strongest language you will find in the Scriptures until you come to the language which the Lord Jesus used in Matthew 23. If you will read that passage in connection with this chapter, you will see that the Lord Jesus topped even Zephaniah in the extreme language of judgment, which He used. It is bloodcurdling, if you please.

We saw in chapter 2 that the judgment of God is worldwide, it is global in its extent, and it includes every nation on the topside of the earth. In verses 1–5 of this chapter, God returns to the judgment that is coming upon His people, and He is very specific. He reveals that the light which a person has will determine the extent of the judgment— in other words, <u>privilege creates responsibility.</u> Your responsibility is measured by the privilege that you have. I like to express it like this: I would rather be a <u>Hottentot in the darkest part of Africa</u> than to be sitting in a Bible-believing church today, hearing the gospel but doing nothing about it. I won't argue about the judgment of the Hottentots in Africa, as that is not what we are talking about here, but I do know what God will do with a person of privilege, one who has had the opportunity of hearing the Word of God and has turned his back upon it. This is very extreme language that is used to express the judgment on Jerusalem, a judgment that is in ratio to her privilege—

JUNGLE
PEOPLE
bountiful

Woe to her that is filthy and polluted, to the oppressing city! [Zeph. 3:1].

17 Aug

<u>Jerusalem was the city</u> in which the temple was located. The priests were there, and the scribes had the Word of God. When wise men

came from the east, seeking the King of the Jews, the scribes had no problem in telling them where the Messiah was to be born, but they simply did not manifest any interest in checking to see if the wise men had any valid information about the Messiah. The scribes knew ✳ the letter of the Law, but that is all they knew. They did not know the Author of the Book, and they were far from Him. God's condemnation of Jerusalem is on the basis of all the light they had.

"Woe to her that is filthy and polluted." This matter of pollution is not something that is new today, but the pollution spoken of here is not physical pollution. This pollution is not on the outside of man; it is on the inside of man. The thing that is causing the pollution on the outside today is that man is polluted and filthy on the inside—that is, before God he is not right.

When a man gets right with God, he is not going to dump his garbage on another man's property, and he is not going to fill a lovely, babbling brook with filth. The ones who are polluting this earth are the godless folk. For example, in one of the beach towns here in Southern California several years ago, there was a meeting of some hippies, a godless crowd. They met in a pasture to hold a protest meeting against pollution. They were decrying the pollution caused by the large factories with their smokestacks which pour out all the dregs and waste materials resulting from industrial production. Very candidly, I agree with them that that's a terrible thing to have taking place. But the interesting thing is that after they held their protest meeting, the city had to spend two thousand dollars to clean up the pasture which those who were protesting pollution had polluted! May I say to you, pollution is on the inside, and when you are godless and wrong with God, you are certainly going to pollute this earth.

Man today is actually wrecking this earth that we are living on, and God's condemnation of Jerusalem is that it is a polluted city, although it was a privileged city, a city that had glorious and wonderful opportunities. This is the picture of that city, but it is also a picture of mankind in general. Notice Paul's verdict in Romans 3:16, "Destruction and misery are in their ways." What a picture of mankind! Man has always left a pile of tin cans and rubbish wherever he has gone on the earth.

Why did God single out the city of Jerusalem? It was a privileged city. This city had the temple of God. It had the Word of God. Therefore, its judgment will be harsher than that of any other city.

God calls Jerusalem not only filthy and polluted, but He also calls it "the oppressing city." It is the oppressing city because of the fact that she did not regard the rights of her people, especially of the poor. She did not consider them; she oppressed the poor.

This is something that I think is so hypocritical in my own government. I am not talking politics now, nor am I speaking of any one party because this is true of the whole structure that we have in Washington, D.C., today. Constantly our congressmen are coming up with programs to help the poor. It is interesting that it is always some rich senator who comes up with such a program. To begin with, he does not know how poor folk feel. He does not know their hardships. Such men have never experienced poverty, and their programs never help the poor; they help some bureaucrats but not the poor. I do not think the poor will ever be helped by any of the plans that men devise. Part of the problem is that the middle-class people are taxed to finance any such program. The middle class are the ones making it possible for the upper class to take our money to help the poor or the lower class. I personally would like to move into one of the other brackets—it would be more comfortable there today. God said that He would judge the city of Jerusalem for their oppression of the poor; so we know how He feels about our oppression.

God is not through with His judgment; He goes on to spell out their sin—

She obeyed not the voice; she received not correction; she trusted not in the Lord; she drew not near to her God [Zeph. 3:2].

"She obeyed not the voice." She was disobedient to God. This city had heard the voice of God but had been disobedient to Him.

"She received not correction." God had sent judgment. One hundred eighty-five thousand Assyrians outside the walls of Jerusalem scared the living daylights out of these people—they were frightened beyond measure (see 2 Kings 18—19). They had been partially judged, but God had let the judgment pass over. You would think that they would have learned their lesson and would have turned to God, but they didn't. Likewise, there are many Christians today who suffer but never learn why God permits it. He never lets anything happen to His own unless there is a purpose back of it. This city, like many of us, "received not correction." She did not learn the lesson.

"She trusted not in the Lord." The city had no trust in Him at all but looked to something else. When the modern nation of Israel celebrated her twentieth anniversary, they displayed this motto: "Science will bring peace to this land." My friend, the Bible says that the Messiah is the Prince of Peace, and He is the only One who can bring peace. But they don't trust Him—they trust science. After that twentieth anniversary, believe me, Israel got into hot water. Science did not bring peace to that land, and my nation has not brought peace to them either.

"She drew not near to her God." Today men are not running to God; they are running from Him as fast as they possibly can. What a picture this is of the city of Jerusalem!

LEADERS,

Her princes within her are roaring lions; her judges are evening wolves; they gnaw not the bones till the morrow [Zeph. 3:3].

"Her princes within her are roaring lions." God is now talking about the leadership of the nation; and, when you speak of judgment, you must talk about the leadership of any nation or city. In my country, when men are running for office, they are always telling us that they are going to think about us, they are going to help us, and they are going to do something for us. So far, as best I can tell, nobody has ever done anything, either from the city level, the state level, or the national level. Why? Because "her princes within her are roaring lions"—they make a big noise.

"Her judges are evening wolves." We have a second meaning for *wolf* today, and I'm not sure but that the Lord included that thought here also. "Her judges are evening wolves"—in other words, they are

CONGRESS

willing to work day and night—not for the people but for themselves. "They gnaw not the bones till the morrow." These men are willing to get all they can. Dr. Charles L. Feinberg comments: "The judges of the people were filled with insatiable greed, devouring all at once in their ravenous hunger. They left nothing till the morning" (*Habakkuk, Zephaniah, Haggai, and Malachi*, p. 64). Many of the men who go into office in our country, promising to help us, have not helped us, but they have done well themselves. By the time they retire from office, many of these men have become well-to-do. This is the thing that God judges. Judah was a nation like ours that had the Word of God. That which is said of Jerusalem could apply to us also. If God spoke out of heaven today, He would have to say these same things concerning us.

ARROGANT

19 AUG '07
SPOKESPERSON
FOR GOD

Her prophets are light and treacherous persons: her priests have polluted the sanctuary, they have done violence to the law [Zeph. 3:4].

"Her prophets are light." This does not mean that they give light! It means that they do not really give the Word of God, but they give a little smattering of psychology with a few Scripture verses put over it like a sugarcoated pill. That's the sort of thing that is being dished out today. They do not talk about judgment or the need for sinners to come to Christ.

"Her prophets are . . . treacherous persons." That is, they are racketeers, religious racketeers. Again, let me suggest that you read Matthew 23 to see if God has changed. You will find there the Lord Jesus' denouncement of religious rulers.

"Her priests have polluted the sanctuary." This is a terrible thing. How have they polluted the sanctuary? They have caused the world outside to lose respect for that which was sacred. By their lives, they brought disrespect upon the temple, upon the sanctuary. The same thing took place in Samuel's day when old Eli was priest. Men no longer had respect for religion. And today men decry the fact that the church has lost its influence. I decry it also, but, very frankly, I do not think that the church deserves the respect of the outside world when we cannot and do not present to them a church that is holy and that is living for God.

"They have done violence to the law." In other words, they did not interpret it accurately. In fact, they did violence to it by omitting the teaching of the Word of God. "The law" here means the total Word of God.

> The just Lord is in the midst thereof; he will not do iniq-
> uity: every morning doth he bring his judgment to light,
> he faileth not; but the unjust knoweth no shame [Zeph.
> 3:5].

"The just Lord is in the midst thereof; he will not do iniquity." God is not going to do evil. The minute that His people do evil while God does nothing, it looks as if God approves that sort of thing. However, God says that He intends to move in judgment—God will not do iniquity.

"Every morning doth he bring his judgment to light, he faileth not; but the unjust knoweth no shame." The unjust simply continue on in sin with no shame at all that is public knowledge.

We have now in verses 6–8 the picture of the Great Tribulation period that is coming in the future, the great Day of the Lord which Zephaniah has talked about. Zephaniah moves from speaking of the city of Jerusalem to talking about the nations of the world in the last days. This is Armageddon, which ends with the return of Christ to earth.

> I have cut off the nations: their towers are desolate: I
> made their streets waste, that none passeth by: their
> cities are destroyed, so that there is no man, that there is
> none inhabitant [Zeph. 3:6].

It has been my privilege to walk through the ruins of great civilizations of the past. Recently, I walked through the ruins of Ostia, the

Surb. of Rome

NOAH - 3000 BC

playground of the Romans. It is just fifteen miles from Rome, but not very well known. It will become well known later, as Rome is developing it, and it will become a tourist attraction. Ostia was where Rome lived it up. It was the Las Vegas of the Roman Empire. As you stand in the ruins of that city and see the stones of the Roman road which were worn by chariot wheels, it is difficult to think that those streets were once crowded and that that city was a great city in its heyday. God says here, "I'm going to make them desolate." It's very difficult to believe that Los Angeles could become that desolate, but it could. It is difficult to believe that New York City could become desolate, but it could.

> I said, Surely thou wilt fear me, thou wilt receive in-
> struction; so their dwelling should not be cut off, howso-
> ever, I punished them: but they rose early, and
> corrupted all their doings [Zeph. 3:7].

The warnings of judgment and the little judgment that did come had no effect upon them. Eventually that will bring down finally the great Day of the Lord, the final time of judgment, which is coming upon this earth.

> Therefore wait ye upon me, saith the Lord, until the day
> that I rise up to the prey: for my determination is to
> gather the nations, that I may assemble the kingdoms, to
> pour upon them mine indignation, even all my fierce
> anger: for all the earth shall be devoured with the fire of
> my jealousy [Zeph. 3:8].

This earth which you and I are living on is moving toward a judgment. Although folk don't believe it, they are moving to judgment. It is this judgment which will be initiated when the Lord Jesus Christ returns to this earth for His church. It begins then with the Great Tribulation period and ends when He comes to establish His Kingdom on this earth.

ALL JUDGMENTS REMOVED AND THE KINGDOM
ESTABLISHED   7 yrs

We are now going to pass from the darkness to the day and to see the blessings which are in store. The storm is over as far as the little Book of Zephaniah is concerned. The book opens with dark forebodings and with ominous rumblings of judgment. The first part of this chapter, which deals with the judgment of the city of Jerusalem, is almost frightening to read. It is frightening when you come to that picture of the Great Tribulation period when God will judge all nations when they are brought up against Jerusalem in that last day (see Zech. 14:1–3). We have seen two kinds of judgment in the Book of Zephaniah. There is God's judgment of His own people, which is always chastisement. "For whom the Lord loveth he chasteneth . . ." (Heb. 12:6)—in other words, He child-trains, or disciplines, them. Then God must judge the unbelieving world also. This is the picture of judgment that is before us in this little book. The Book of Zephaniah is like a Florida hurricane, a Texas tornado, a Mississippi River flood, a Minnesota snowstorm, and a California earthquake all rolled into one.

As you read this book you might think that God hates His people and that He hates mankind in general; you might think that He is vindictive, cruel, and brutal, that He is unfeeling and unmoved. However, the little story that I told in the Introduction is the story that illustrates the message of Zephaniah. It is the story of the man who took a little child into the darkness of the night and rushed her away from home. It looked as if he were kidnapping the child. It was frightful when he turned her over to another man who plunged a knife into her abdomen. But when you know the whole story, you find that the man was the father of that little girl. His own precious little girl had been having attacks of appendicitis, and that night he picked her up and rushed her to the hospital to put her into the hands of the family physician. Everything was done in tenderness. We find today that our Great Physician takes His own, the ones He loves, and puts them on the operating table. Even in judgment, God is love. When He is judging the unsaved or when He is judging those who are His own, God is love.

Someday the final curtain is coming down on this world in which we live. Man's little day will be over, and judgment will come for lost mankind. But God will restore His children, and we will find out that what we endured down here was actually a blessing in disguise. Let me tell you another little story, one that actually happened. It is the story of a boy who was away from home in school, and things got rough for him there. The lessons were difficult, and he was homesick. He wrote home and said, "Dad, it's hard here. The assignments are too heavy, and the dormitory rules are too strict. I'm homesick and I want to come home." The father wrote back a stern and severe letter in which he said, "You stay on there and study hard. Apply yourself to your work." When the boy got that letter, he thought, *I don't think my dad loves me anymore. My dad couldn't love me, or he wouldn't want me to go through this torture that I'm going through here.* We have a heavenly Father who tells us, "You stay down there in the college of life. I'm preparing a place for you, and I am also preparing you for that place." With this in mind, let us turn to this final passage of Zephaniah.

> **For then will I turn to the people a pure language, that they may all call upon the name of the LORD, to serve him with one consent [Zeph. 3:9].**

God has this far-off purpose—it is called the teleological purpose of God. We will find it all through this section because now we are in the light. We are no longer in the darkness of the judgment, no longer in the Day of the Lord which begins at night. The sun has now arisen, and light has broken upon mankind.

"For then will I turn to the people a pure language." He does not mean that everybody is going to speak Hebrew, although a great many people think that that is the meaning. Nor is He going to turn them to some other, perhaps unknown, language which everybody will speak. Nor is the "pure language" English spoken with a Texas accent! Many people find my Texas accent rather distasteful. I thought for awhile that you were going to have to get accustomed to it because it was what everybody would be speaking in heaven—but this doesn't mean that at all. "Pure language" means exactly what it says: the language will be pure. There will be no blasphemy heard. There will be no vileness nor vulgarity. There will be nothing repulsive. The language will be pure.

At one time we had a neighbor who was a very big-hearted woman in many ways, but she was unsaved. She not only had a mean tongue, but she also had the vilest tongue that I have ever heard. It was offensive to people whenever she would lose her temper, for you could hear her throughout the entire neighborhood. It was very distasteful, so much so that some wanted to report her. In heaven, my friend, there will be nobody to report because there is going to be a pure language. Heaven will be pure in thought, word, and deed.

"That they may all call upon the name of the Lord, to serve him with one consent." There will be no rebellion against God in that day. Heaven is going to be a really nice nieghborhood to live in. In fact, it is going to be a glorious place, and you are going to have some good neighbors there.

From beyond the rivers of Ethiopia my suppliants, even the daughter of my dispersed, shall bring mine offering [Zeph. 3:10].

26 Aug '07

This verse of Scripture has been variously translated, and all sorts of interpretations have been presented for it. One interpretation is that the ark of the covenant is down in Ethiopia and that it will be brought up to Jerusalem as an offering at this time. I do not think that that is the thing Zephaniah has in mind here at all. Others call attention to a tribe in Ethiopia or Abyssinia known as the *Falashas*, which comes from the same root as the word *Philistine*, meaning migrant. They claim that they can trace their origin back to Israel, that they are Israelites. It is argued that these are the "suppliants" referred to here. Many feel that this verse speaks of those converted from the nations of the world who will bring dispersed Israelites back to their land as an offering to the Lord. My position is that this verse means that Ethiopia will enter the millennial Kingdom—that is what is important for us to see. The offering that they will bring is the sacrifice of Christ Himself; in other words, they will come, having accepted His redemption.

HARAN
26 AUG '07

> **In that day shalt thou not be ashamed for all thy doings, wherein thou hast transgressed against me: for then I will take away out of the midst of thee them that rejoice in thy pride, and thou shalt no more be haughty because of my holy mountain [Zeph. 3:11].**

JUDGED BY OUR ACTIONS

God is talking to His own here. We have seen that one of the things for which God was judging them was that there was no shame in their vile acts and gross immorality—they were not ashamed of it. But, my friend, God's people will never reach the place where they can be satisfied in sin. If you can live in sin and be happy—you can be sure of one thing—you are not a child of God. The prodigal son was never happy in the pigpen, and since he was the son of the father, he *had* to say, "I'm going home to my father." That revealed that he wasn't a pig. Pigs love pigpens, but sons don't love pigpens. A son wants to go to the father's house because he has the nature of the father. God makes this very clear here: "In that day shalt thou not be ashamed for all thy doings, wherein thou hast transgressed against me."

"For then I will take away out of the midst of thee them that rejoice in thy pride, and thou shalt no more be haughty because of my holy mountain." This speaks of the day when the meek shall inherit the earth. The other crowd has it now, and they are not doing very well with it.

MILLENNIUM

> **I will also leave in the midst of thee an afflicted and poor people, and they shall trust in the name of the LORD [Zeph. 3:12].**

606 587 597   *606 584 597*

When the Babylonians took Judah into captivity, there were three deportations of slaves taken, but they never took all of the people. The poor, the afflicted, and the crippled were not taken to Babylon. You can imagine how they felt. It was terrible to go into Babylonian captivity to become a slave, but it was actually worse to be left behind. God says here, "I intend to take care of the afflicted and the poor." You will notice that all the way through Scripture, the Lord often mentions the fact that He intends someday to see that the poor get an honest deal and that they are treated right. The only one in the world today who has a helpful program for the poor is the Lord Jesus Christ. If you are poor and needy, He is the one to go to. He can help you, and He is the only one who can help.

The remnant of Israel shall not do iniquity, nor speak lies; neither shall a deceitful tongue be found in their mouth: for they shall feed and lie down, and none shall make them afraid [Zeph. 3:13].

"The remnant of Israel shalt not do iniquity." God has always had a remnant, and there will be this very large remnant in the Millennium.

"Nor speak lies; neither shall a deceitful tongue be found in their mouth." That the day is coming when they will not do these things would seem to indicate that they once did them. Even God's people indulged in sin—but not permanently. They cannot continue to live in sin. They may get their feet dirty, they may get down in the pigpen, but they simply will not stay in the pigpen.

"For they shall feed and lie down, and none shall make them afraid." All of this has reference to the day when God will put His people back in their land and give them the land. Therefore, are you prepared to say that what has happened and is happening in that land today is a fulfillment of prophecy? Is it true that "none shall make them afraid"? My friend, Israel has not had a moment, since they've been in that land, that they have not been frightened.

We come now to a description of the day when the King is going to set up His Kingdom on the earth.

Sing, O daughter of Zion; shout, O Israel; be glad and rejoice with all the heart, O daughter of Jerusalem.

> The LORD hath taken away thy judgments, he hath cast
> out thine enemy: the king of Israel, even the LORD, is in
> the midst of thee: thou shalt not see evil any more [Zeph.
> 3:14-15].

The Lord Jesus will come to the earth, evil will be put down, and ". . .
the earth shall be full of the knowledge of the LORD, as the waters cover
the sea" (Isa. 11:9).

> In that day it shall be said to Jerusalem, Fear thou not:
> and to Zion, Let not thine hands be slack [Zeph. 3:16].

"In that day it shall be said to Jerusalem, Fear thou not." Jerusalem has
reason to be afraid now, but she will have nothing to fear in that day.

"And to Zion, Let not thine hands be slack." In other words, "Be
busy for the Lord."

Verse 17 is a marvelous verse—

> The LORD thy God in the midst of thee is mighty; he will
> save, he will rejoice over thee with joy; he will rest in his
> love, he will joy over thee with singing [Zeph. 3:17].

My friend, God has a purpose. He goes through the night of judgment
in order to bring us into the light of a new day. He does all of this that
the day might come when He can rest in His love. God loves you and
me today. I don't know about you, but I doubt very seriously whether
He can rest in His love for Vernon McGee. He could say of me, "He's
not perfected yet. He seems so immature. He is so filled with faults.
He is apt to digress, apt to detour, at any moment." God cannot rest in
His love today. But the day is coming when we will be in His
likeness—after He has put us on the "operating table". Then He is
going to bring us to Himself. What a wonderful and glorious picture
this is!

I will gather them that are sorrowful for the solemn assembly, who are of thee, to whom the reproach of it was a burden.

Behold, at that time I will undo all that afflict thee: and I will save her that halteth, and gather her that was driven out; and I will get them praise and fame in every land where they have been put to shame.

At that time will I bring you again, even in the time that I gather you: for I will make you a name and a praise among all people of the earth, when I turn back your captivity before your eyes, saith the LORD [Zeph. 3:18–20].

Oh, this is the day of light that will come. It will be glorious for the nation Israel, and it will be glorious for the church also. God is putting many of us through the furnace, and He is putting us through trials. The glorious thing about heaven will not be the golden streets, it will not be the gates of pearl, and it will not be the fact that He is going to wipe away all tears. The glorious thing in heaven will be that we are going to thank Him for every trial we had and for every burden that He put on us in this life.

I conclude with this wonderful little poem, "In the Crucible"—

> Out from the mine and the darkness,
> Out from the damp and the mold,
> Out from the fiery furnace,
> Cometh each grain of gold.
> Crushed into atoms and leveled
> Down to the humblest dust
> With never a heart to pity,
> With never a hand to trust.
>
> Molten and hammered and beaten,
> Seemeth it ne'er to be done.

Oh! for such fiery trial,
What hath the poor gold done?
Oh! 'twere a mercy to leave it
Down in the damp and the mold.
If this is the glory of living,
Then better to be dross than gold.

Under the press and the roller,
Into the jaws of the mint,
Stamped with the emblem of freedom
With never a flaw or a dint.
Oh! what a joy the refining
Out of the damp and the mold!
And stamped with the glorious image,
Oh, beautiful coin of gold!

Someday, when you and I are in the presence of our Savior, we will thank Him for every burden, every trial, every heartache. We will thank Him for dealing with us as a wise father deals with his children, and we will thank Him for the dark side of His love.

BIBLIOGRAPHY

(Recommended for Further Study)

Feinberg, Charles L. *The Minor Prophets*. Chicago, Illinois: Moody Press, 1976.

Gaebelein, Arno C. *The Annotated Bible*. 1917. Reprint. Neptune, New Jersey: Loizeaux Brothers, 1971.

Ironside, H. A. *The Minor Prophets*. Neptune, New Jersey: Loizeaux Brothers, n.d.

Jensen, Irving L. *Minor Prophets of Judah*. Chicago, Illinois: Moody Press, 1975. (Obadiah, Joel, Micah, Nahum, Zephaniah, and Habakkuk.)

Unger, Merrill F. *Unger's Commentary on the Old Testament*, Vol. 2. Chicago, Illinois: Moody Press, 1982.

HAGGAI

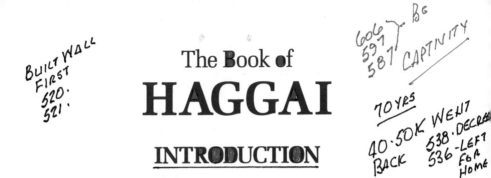

The Book of
HAGGAI

INTRODUCTION

The prophets to the returned remnant were Haggai, Zechariah, and Malachi. Haggai, the writer of this short book, is mentioned in Ezra 5:1–2 and 6:14 as one of the two prophets who encouraged the remnant (that returned after the Babylonian captivity) to rebuild the temple in spite of the difficulties that beset them on every hand. From this and the brief references that he made to himself in his prophecy, four things become apparent:

1. <u>Haggai was self-effacing—he exalted the Lord</u>. He took the same position that John the Baptist took: "<u>He must increase, but I must decrease</u>" (John 3:30).

2. He was God's messenger. The expression "<u>Thus saith the Lord</u>" characterizes his message.

3. He not only rebuked the people; he also cheered and encouraged them in a marvelous way.

4. He not only preached; he also practiced.

Haggai begins his book by saying, "<u>In the second year of Darius the king, in the sixth month, in the first day of the month</u>." Hystaspes (the Darius mentioned here) began to reign in 521 B.C., making the second year of his reign about 520 B.C. "The second year of Darius" enables the historian to pinpoint the time of this prophet in profane history. <u>It is interesting to note that the post-Captivity prophets begin</u> ✳ <u>to date their prophecies according to the reign of gentile rulers</u>. Those prophets who prophesied before the Captivity always tied the dates of their writings into the reign of either a king of Israel or a king of Judah or both. <u>After the Captivity, since there was no king in either the</u>

northern or the southern kingdom, Haggai dates his prophecy according to a gentile king. The Lord Jesus said, ". . . Jerusalem shall be trodden down of the Gentiles, until the times of the Gentiles be fulfilled" (Luke 21:24). In Haggai's day the "times of the Gentiles" had already begun (in fact, it began with the captivity of Judah under Nebuchadnezzar). Since that time Jerusalem has been under gentile domination, and Haggai dates his prophecy accordingly.

The theme of Haggai is the temple. The reconstruction and refurbishing of the temple were the supreme passion of this prophet. He not only rebuked the people for their delay in rebuilding the temple, but he also encouraged them and helped them in this enterprise.

Haggai constantly referred to the "word of the Lord" as the supreme authority. He willingly humbled himself that the Lord might be exalted. His message was practical. It was as simple and factual as $2+2=4$. The prophecy of Haggai and the Epistle of James have much in common. Both put the emphasis upon the daily grind. Action is spiritual. A "do nothing" attitude is wicked. Both place this yardstick down upon life. Work is the measure of life.

Haggai's contemporary, Zechariah, was visionary and had his head in the clouds, but pragmatic Haggai had both feet on the ground. The man of action and the dreamer need to walk together. First Corinthians 15:58 can appropriately be written over this book: "Therefore, my beloved brethren, be ye stedfast, unmoveable, always abounding in the work of the Lord, forasmuch as ye know that your labour is not in vain in the Lord."

There are two keys verses in this book: "Go up to the mountain, and bring wood, and build the house; and I will take pleasure in it, and I will be glorified, saith the Lord. . . . And the Lord stirred up the spirit of Zerubbabel the son of Shealtiel, governor of Judah, and the spirit of Joshua the son of Josedech, the high priest, and the spirit of all the remnant of the people; and they came and did work in the house of the Lord of hosts, their God" (Hag. 1:8, 14).

606 BC
DANIEL

OUTLINE

The compass of this book is three months and fourteen days, according to the calendar. There are five messages in the book, and each was given on a specific date. The calendar furnishes the clue for the contents.

I. **September 1, 520 B.C., Chapter 1:1–11**
   A Challenge to the People
   A. A Charge of Conflict of Interest, Chapter 1:1–4
   B. A Call to Consider Their Ways, Chapter 1:5–7
   C. A Command to Construct the Temple, Chapter 1:8–11

II. **September 24, 520 B.C., Chapter 1:12–15**
   The Response to the Challenge
   A. Construction of the Temple; People Obeyed, Chapter 1:12
   B. Confirmation from God, Chapter 1:13–15

III. **October 21, 520 B.C., Chapter 2:1–9**
   The Discouragement of the People; The Encouragement of the Lord

IV. **December 24, 520 B.C., Chapter 2:10–19**
   An Appeal to the Law; The Explanation of the Principle

V. **December 24, 520 B.C., Chapter 2:20–23**
   A Revelation of God's Program; An Expectation for the Future

CHAPTER 1

THEME: *Challenge to the people; charge of conflict of interest; call to consider their ways; command to construct the temple; construction of the temple— obedience of the people; confirmation from God*

Haggai was a prophet to the restored remnant who returned to Jerusalem after the seventy-year captivity in Babylon. In the study of this Israel we will note how important it is to consider the historical books along with the prophectic books. There is a little cluster of books that belong together: Ezra, Nehemiah, and Esther for the historical record; and Haggai, Zechariah, and Malachi for the prophectic section—also, the Book of Daniel probably should be studied first. These books belong together and constitute a unit.

CHALLENGE TO THE PEOPLE

Haggai and Zechariah prophesied during the same period, yet their approach was altogether different. They both challenged and encouraged the returned remnant to rebuild the temple and then to rebuild the walls of Jerusalem. "Then the prophets, Haggai the prophet, and Zechariah the son of Iddo, prophesied unto the Jews that were in Judah and Jerusalem in the name of the God of Israel, even unto them. Then rose up Zerubbabel the son of Shealtiel, and Jeshua the son of Jozadak, and began to build the house of God which is at Jerusalem: and with them were the prophets of God helping them" (Ezra 5:1–2). So, you see, both Haggai and Zechariah are mentioned in this historical Book of Ezra as the two prophets who encouraged the people to rebuild the temple and also aided them in it. Also, in Ezra 6:14 we read: "And the elders of the Jews builded, and they prospered through the prophesying of Haggai the prophet and Zechariah the son of Iddo. And they builded, and finished it, according to the commandment of the God of Israel, and according to the commandment of Cyrus, and Darius, and Artaxerxes king of Persia."

PERSIAN

330 BC ALEXANDER TAKES PERSIA
542 BC

CHARGE OF CONFLICT OF INTEREST

**In the second year of Darius the king, in the sixth
month, in the first day of the month, came the word of
the Lord by Haggai the prophet unto Zerubbabel the son
of Shealtiel, governor of Judah, and to Joshua the son of
Josedech, the high priest, saying [Hag. 1:1].**

"In the second year of Darius the king, in the sixth month, in the first
day of the month" gives us the date of this prophecy, which is September 1, 520 B.C. according to the Jewish calendar. This is a book we can
date very easily. As we said in the Introduction, the dating is according to the gentile ruler, Darius. The dating is no longer geared to the
king of Israel or Judah because Haggai is writing during the "times of
the Gentiles," which began with the Babylonian captivity and continues to the present day. The Lord Jesus said, "And they shall fall by
the edge of the sword, and shall be led away captive into all nations:
and Jerusalem shall be trodden down of the Gentiles, until the times
of the Gentiles be fulfilled" (Luke 21:24).

"Came the word of the Lord by Haggai the prophet." We will find
all the way through this little book that Haggai repeatedly refers to the
Word of the Lord. He is making it clear that he is not speaking his own
thoughts but is giving the Word of God to his people.

"Unto Zerubbabel the son of Shealtiel, governor of Judah." The
name *Zerubbabel* means "sown in Babylon"; that is, he was born in
captivity down in Babylon. It is actually a heathen name, by the way.
He was in the line of David, the grandson of Jehoiachin (see 1 Chron.
3:16–19), and was appointed by Cyrus to be governor of Judah.

"And to Joshua the son of Josedech, the high priest." Joshua was
the son of Jehozadak who was high priest at the time of the Babylonian
invasion (see 1 Chron. 6:15). This man was the religious head. So,
you see, God is sending His message first to the leaders, the religious
and civil rulers.

When the Israelites returned from Babylonian captivity to their
own land, they returned with great anticipation, and their enthusiasm
for rebuilding ran high. But they met gigantic obstacles which re-

quired herculean effort and hardships. After they had gone through a period like that, they were discouraged when they began to build the temple. The difficulties seemed insurmountable. Therefore they rationalized and decided that it was not the time to build. In other words, this was their pseudoconsolation. They decided to maintain the status quo. They said, "It is so hard, evidently God doesn't intend us to do it." They had laid the foundation of the temple, but the opposition of the Samaritans was so intense that they simply stopped building, and their excuse was, "Well, the time has not come."

Thus speaketh the Lord of hosts, saying, This people say. The time is not come, the time that the Lord's house should be built [Hag. 1:2].

If you will read the Book of Nehemiah, you will see that, when they were rebuilding the walls of Jerusalem, the opposition was terrific. Well, they had the same kind of opposition in rebuilding the temple, and the people said, "Well, this is not the Lord's time to build it."

Notice that God says, "This people say"—ordinarily He calls them My people, but not here. By this He doesn't mean that He has disowned them; He is just displeased with them. They are not in His will, and they are covering their disobedience with the pious sounding excuse, "It is just not the right time to build the Lord's house."

What Haggai is going to say will hurt a little. He is going to stick the knife in the trouble spot that, by the way, touches the lives of many Christians. Have you ever heard people say that they had given up trying to do something or that they did not go someplace because it was not the Lord's will? They will sometimes say that the Lord directed them to do something else. Saying that it is the Lord's will to do this or not to do that is a Christian cliché that covers a multitude of sins. It is so easy, when things get hard and rough, to turn in a report to everyone that says, "The Lord wanted me to do something else." Many a preacher, when things got tough in his church, has said, "The Lord needs me somewhere else." My heart goes out to pastors who are really trying to serve God but are having trouble and end up saying,

"The Lord is leading me elsewhere." When the Lord's people started building the temple and the going got rough, they said, "It's not the Lord's time to build."

I remember when we attempted to remodel the church in downtown Los Angeles, California, where I served as pastor. The church in its long history had never been remodeled, and the seats, which numbered four thousand, were built to take care of people who lived fifty or sixty years ago. We discovered that people today are about 2½ inches wider than they were fifty years ago! We decided to put in new cushioned seats. Some of the very pious folk said, "We don't feel that money should be spent for cushions. We should give that money to missions." Now the majority of the people wanted the cushioned seats, and I did too, so I made a proposition to the congregation. I said, "There are so many people enthusiastic about remodeling that they are going to give enough money to cushion their seat and yours too, so those of you who don't want to pay for cushioned seats can give your twenty-five dollars to missions. I hope that we can take an offering today for several hundred twenty-five dollar checks." Well, there were very few twenty-five dollar checks. Why? The truth was that the folk who were objecting to the cushioned seats never intended to give at all, and "missions instead of cushions" was their excuse. But what they *said* was, "It isn't God's will to have cushioned seats. The time hasn't come to remodel the church."

It was my privilege to remodel every church which I served as pastor. I never built a new church, but I remodeled each of them. And I always encountered the same problem. In each church there was a little group—a very small group, thank God for that—which didn't *do* anything, but they were good at criticizing. And the excuse was always the same—"The money shouldn't be spent on us here; it should go to missions." Then they should have given it to missions, but they did not.

The crowd that Haggai is addressing rationalized in the same way. He is pulling the Band-Aid off and exposing the sore. And it isn't an "ouchless" Band-Aid—it *hurts*, you may be sure of that.

Now here is message number one, given on September 1, 520 B.C. Notice that Haggai is giving the *Word* of the Lord.

> Then came the word of the LORD by Haggai the prophet,
> saying,
>
> Is it time for you, O ye, to dwell in your ceiled houses,
> and this house lie waste? [Hag. 1:3–4].

These folk who said it was not time to build the Lord's house had all built their *own* houses—it seemed the time to do that! And the Lord pointed out that their houses were "ceiled houses." This means that they were beautifully paneled; they were luxuriously built. And for fifteen years, while they had been building their elaborate homes, the Lord's house had been lying waste.

It is amazing, but I have found it true throughout my many years in the ministry, that a great many people say, "I feel it is God's will for me to help you in your ministry," and then when the going gets a little rough, say, "It doesn't seem to be the Lord's will for me to help at this time." You see, the minute that things become difficult, that is the time most people decide their resolve is not the Lord's will. But when it is something for their own selfish ends, they usually go ahead and do it, don't they? Most people are that way. We make the effort to accomplish that which will always be to our advantage.

In Haggai's day, how in the world were the people able to build their lovely paneled homes? Surely they encountered difficulties, but they were not willing to face the same difficulties to build the Lord's house. Their lame excuse was, "It's just not the Lord's will right now for us to do that."

Oh, I get so weary of hearing people give that excuse for not doing something for God! What do they know about the Lord's will? Just because something is difficult and hard and is going to cost you something, does that mean it is not the Lord's will? May I say to you, that is *not* the way to interpret the Lord's will. Sometimes the Lord's will is very rugged. If we could just listen to the stories of some of God's choice saints of the past, they would tell us that God's will was not always a smooth path.

I wonder what Abraham would say to the people today who say, "It is not God's will for me to do this or that." Abraham lived in Ur of the

Chaldees. This man who was to be the father of the Israelites was no doubt a good businessman. He had a nice business in Ur, a highly civilized city in those days and a prosperous one. It was a city of luxury. One day God said to Abraham, "I want you to leave Ur." It would have been easy for Abraham to rationalize, "I must have misunderstood the Lord. He would not ask me to leave this place. The life here is soft and easy. It couldn't be the Lord's will for me to leave this city."

There are literally thousands of missionaries on the mission field today who are making great sacrifices. Why? They do it because they believe it is God's will for them to be on the mission field. I wonder how many of us here at home should be on the mission field. I wonder how many church members there are today who are as busy as termites arranging social events that require no sacrifice or hardship, instead of standing up to the opposition and really getting out the Word of God.

Notice again that Haggai is making it clear that these are not his own words; they are the words of *God*.

I always feel bad when I am in a place like Mexico, and I see all of those ornate cathedrals and the people living in poverty around them. It is easy for us to point a finger and say, "That just isn't right." I agree that it isn't right, but neither is it right for a church to be in a state of disrepair. A church needs to be attractive in order to attract the sinner. One excuse I heard for a church being in such terrible shape was that the congregation gave all of its money to missions. A deacon in that church told me that the reason their church did not have a carpet on the floor or new pews was that all their money had gone to missions. When that deacon took me to his home, he treated me royally. He put me in a guest room that was nicer than any room I had ever been in. His home, I was told, cost over one hundred thousand dollars back in the old days. I have a notion it is worth a great deal more today. It was all I could do to keep quiet. I had to bite my tongue to keep from saying, "You believe in giving to missions, and you don't put a rug on the floor of your church, but look at your home! You could have been a little less lavish and still could have had money for missions *and* your church."

Let me ask you a question, friend: "How much are you spending on yourself, and how much are you doing for God?" That question gets close to us, doesn't it?

May I use another illustration concerning this subject? I went to dinner with a friend of mine who is a fine Christian layman. The dinner was rather expensive, and he left a generous tip for the waitress. Then we went to a church service that evening in order to hear a certain preacher. We heard a good sermon, and when the offering plate was passed, my friend put in one dollar, which was much less than he had given the waitress. I thought, *My, he's not even tipping God!* My friend, this gets right down to where we live.

The Israelites were saying, "It is just not the time for the Lord's house to be built." God says, "Then why is it time for *your* houses to be built?" There is a lot of hypocrisy in the church today. It is sickening to hear people boast about what they do for God when what they do for themselves is a thousand times more than what they are doing for God.

I told you that what Haggai has to say will hurt. He would never win a popularity contest. He is rather like an alarm clock. The alarm clock will never become the most treasured possession of the average American. It is an institution for our contemporary American society but not one that will win a loving cup or a popularity contest. We do not like to be awakened from a sound and restful sleep. The culprit who does it is a criminal, and he should be punished, not rewarded. There are manufacturers today who are making alarm clocks with pleasant sounds, but they are still alarm clocks. Today America is prosperous and powerful and comfortable and satisfied and satiated. We have come to a place where it is woe to anyone who disturbs us, sounds an alarm, blows a whistle, or turns on a siren. In one community a church was restrained from putting up chimes because it would wake up the people in the neighborhood on Sunday morning. If Paul Revere rode again today, he would be arrested for disturbing the peace. John the Baptist would lose his head, not for rebuking a king's sinful life but for being a rabble-rouser and a calamity-howler.

That is the reason God's prophets never won a popularity contest. They were stoned, not starred. And Haggai is an alarm clock. He wakes us up, and he disturbs us. We don't like that. And the people in his day didn't like it. They had just come out of the Babylonian captivity, and they didn't want to hear his message. Haggai occupied a very difficult position. He stood between a rock and a hard place. Yet he attempted to wake up his people to do something for God, and his method was very unusual, though not original by any means. Although his method is not being used in our day, I think it would still be effective in God's work.

CALL TO CONSIDER THEIR WAYS

Now God calls their attention to something which is very practical. This gets right down to the nitty-gritty of life.

> **Now therefore thus saith the Lord of hosts; Consider your ways [Hag. 1:5].**

"Consider your ways" is literally, set your heart upon your ways. Look at what is happening to you. Now He goes into detail—

> **Ye have sown much, and bring in little; ye eat, but ye have not enough; ye drink, but ye are not filled with drink; ye clothe you, but there is none warm; and he that earneth wages earneth wages to put it into a bag with holes.**
>
> **Thus saith the Lord of hosts; Consider your ways [Hag. 1:6–7].**

God was judging them concerning their material things, and they were not recognizing it as His judgment. We see in the Book of Hebrews, "If ye endure chastening, God dealeth with you as with sons; for what son is he whom the father chasteneth not?" (Heb. 12:7). When God disciplines us, there is a reason for it. The child of God needs to consider his ways. He needs to examine his own heart to see why God is putting him through the mill or using sandpaper on him. God wants to smooth the rough edges off our lives; so He does use sandpaper.

For the people of Israel there had been crop failure. There had been famine. There had been little money to buy clothes or food, and they had no savings account. But they never once attributed this to their disobedience. They were trying to explain it in other ways. What about God's children in our day? "Oh," they say, "that's just my luck." It is not *luck* if you are God's child. Difficulties come to you for a purpose. God won't let anything happen to you unless it has a purpose. God is trying to develop something valuable in your heart and life. That is why God said, "consider your ways." Man's ways always seem right to him. The writer of the Book of Proverbs says, "There is a way which seemeth right unto a man, but the end thereof are the ways of death" (Prov. 14:12). In Isaiah 53:6 we read, "All we like sheep have gone astray; we have turned every one to his *own* way . . ." (italics mine). The problem with mankind today is that we will want to go our own way. Again the writer of Psalm 1 says, "For the LORD knoweth the way of the righteous: but the way of the ungodly shall perish" (Ps. 1:6).

Notice how the Word of God enlarges upon the things that reveal man's way as opposed to God's way: Let the wicked forsake his way, and the unrighteous man his thoughts: and let him return unto the LORD, and he will have mercy upon him; and to our God, for he will abundantly pardon" (Isa. 55:7). And in Proverbs 13:15 He says that ". . . the way of transgressors is hard." It certainly is hard! Again in Isaiah He says, "For as the heavens are higher than the earth, so are my ways higher than your ways, and my thoughts than your thoughts" (Isa. 55:9). And then—"O LORD, I know that the way of man is not in himself: it is not in man that walketh to direct his steps" (Jer. 10:23). Also, "Thus saith the LORD, Stand ye in the ways, and see, and ask for the old paths, where is the good way, and walk therein, and ye shall find rest for your souls. But they said, We will not walk therein" (Jer. 6:16). Man is in rebellion against God. In Jeremiah 10:2 God says, ". . . Learn not the way of the heathen. . . ." And God says, ". . . This is the way, walk ye in it . . ." (Isa. 30:21). And the Lord Jesus said, "Verily, verily, I say unto you, He that entereth not by the door into the sheepfold, but climbeth up some other way, the same is a thief and a robber. But he that entereth in by the door is the shepherd of the sheep" (John 10:1–2). He goes on to say, "I am the door: by me if any man enter in, he shall be saved, and shall go in and out, and find pasture" (John 10:9). How tremendous this is!

This is what God is saying to His people. He wants them to consider their *ways*. He wants them to set their hearts upon their ways. He asks, "Don't you see what is happening to you?"

Now let me ask you, "What *way* are you on today? What path are you taking? Where is that path leading you? Have you ever considered where drugs are going to lead you? It is a broad way where you start out, and you can do as you please, but that broad way is actually a funnel, and it grows narrower and narrower until there is only one little opening, which leads only to destruction. But God says that the way which leads to life is a narrow way—Christ is that way; He is the *only* way to the Father. When you enter the narrow way, it becomes broader and broader as you go along until you can go in and out and find pasture. You will have life and have it abundantly. My friend, it is time to consider your ways. Set your heart upon your ways. Where are you headed today? How is your marriage working out? If you are a young person in college, do you have a goal in life? If you are a young lady, how about the young man you are dating? Where is he leading you? What is going to happen to you? Why don't you consider your ways?

Folk from all walks of life write to me. Many are headed in the right direction; others very frankly say that they are on the wrong path, and they are suffering broken homes, broken hearts, and wrecked lives. God says, "Consider your ways."

COMMAND TO CONSTRUCT THE TEMPLE

Now God is going to give them the solution to their problems. It is so simple, so clear that you may wonder why it is necessary to emphasize it. God gives them a command to construct the temple, and He tells them three things that they are to do. You see, the children of Israel had a conflict of interests. They had put their own homes before God's house. They were putting their selfish ends ahead of God's program. The Lord Jesus, in the Sermon on the Mount, said that we are to seek first the Kingdom of God and His righteousness (see Matt. 6:33). That "righteousness" is in Christ. When you have Christ, you have everything—you have all those things you are after. Money can be spiritual, depending on what you use it for. Your home can be spiritual if it is a place where God is honored. It can be a place where a testimony for the Lord is given, where friends can come and be refreshed, or where a Bible class can be taught. It can be a place as sacred as your church. The things that people are after today may not be wrong, but it is wrong when they put them *first* in their lives and use them for their own selfish ends.

Now God tells the people in Haggai's day what they are to do:

✳ **Go up to the mountain, and bring wood, and build the house; and I will take pleasure in it, and I will be glorified, saith the LORD [Hag. 1:8].**

The solution is so simple—there are only three things they are to do: (1) "Go up to the mountain, and" (2) "bring wood, and" (3) "build the house." I'll be honest with you, I wonder why some of the children of Israel had not realized this sooner. When people get that big "I" in front of their eyes, it obscures everything else, and they are blind to the things they should see. That which should be very simple becomes a very complex problem. People today say, "Life is so complicated. We need a psychiatrist. We need to get things straightened out." My friend, if you just put God in His rightful place, He will straighten out a great many things for you. But first, you must get the big "I" out of the way.

"Go up to the mountain, and bring wood." If you have visited the land of Israel, you may wonder about God's command to go up to the mountain and bring down trees since that land is almost denuded of trees today. For many years now Israel has been carrying on a project of tree planting. Although they have planted millions of trees, the hills still look bare to me. Very few of them have any sign of green on them. At one time that land was covered with trees, as this verse reveals. God wouldn't tell them to go up to the mountain and get wood if there were not wood up there. Then what happened to the trees?

Well, when the enemy invaded Israel in A.D. 70, the forces of Rome not only destroyed the cities, they also denuded the land of trees. They cut down practically every tree.

Now notice again God's simple solution to their problems: (1) "Go up to the mountain, and" (2) "bring wood, and" (3) "build the house." Going up to the mountain, felling the trees, and making them into lumber would take work and a great deal of effort.

My friend, if you are not ready to go to work for the Lord, if you are not willing to do what God wants you to do—whatever that might be—Bible study is really not going to help you very much. God believes in work, and the message of this little Book of Haggai is the gospel of work.

As we have seen in this marvelous little book, first there was God's challenge to His people. They were kidding themselves that they were doing God's will. But the reason they had not built the temple was that they were just plain lazy. They tried to conceal that fact with the very pious platitude, "The time isn't right. It isn't the will of God to build at this time." God told them to get off their haunches and go to work. He said, "You have been attributing the fact that you have had bad crops and that things are difficult for you to other causes. You have been blaming your circumstances. Why don't you blame Me? I am the One who has sent trouble to you. I'm trying to wake you up." He tells them to consider their ways, to set their hearts on their ways. And now He says to get busy. He charged them with a conflict of interests, then He called them to consider their ways, and now He commands them to start to build the temple. And it is very simple, "Go to the mountain and bring down wood. You can't expect the logs to roll down to you. It is up to you to go to work."

There are so many voices today encouraging Christians to expect a miracle in their lives. They say, "God is going to deal with you by a miracle!" Well, I'm here to tell you that He is not. It would have been very easy for someone to have come along and to have told these Israelites to expect a miracle, but God says, "Go up there and bring down wood. Go to work." My friend, there is no easy shortcut in our service for God.

Very frankly, laziness is the reason Sunday school teachers don't succeed. Laziness is the reason preachers don't succeed. Laziness is the reason people fail in their Christian lives. You have to *work* at it. I do not think that the Holy Spirit will ever bless laziness.

In seminary I remember one of the students complaining to the professor, "Doctor, that book you assigned for us to read is really *dry!*" The professor looked up and smiled, "Well, dampen it with a little sweat from your brow." That's the way to do it, friend. Don't expect the Christian life to be handed to you on a silver platter. The miracle comes in the work that you do. God told His people in Haggai's day to go to work.

Dr. Frank Morgan has called it (1) the *appeal to the mind*. God told them at the very beginning, "You say it is not time to build God's house? I want you to *think* about that. How is it that *you* are living in fine houses?" That was His appeal to the mind. (2) He *appealed to the heart*. He called them to consider, to set their heart on this. They had not done so, but that was His challenge. (3) God gave them a command, and that command was an *appeal to the will*. "Go up, bring wood, and build"—so simple yet so important.

My friend, roll up your sleeves, and let's go to work for God today. So many people are sitting on the sidelines. This is a day of spectator sports; but frankly, it is a day of spectator Christians also. They like to sit on the sidelines and watch somebody else do it. Many a preacher is being worked to death. He is called upon to visit all the sick folk in his congregation. He does all the administrative work—he is expected to supervise everything. What about you deacons? Why don't you go to work? What about you members of the church? Are you visiting the sick? The pastor is to train you to do the work of the ministry. He is not the one to do it all. The work should be divided and shared. The burden of the ministry should not fall on just a few folk. If you are a member of a local congregation, you should go to work. Work is something which is desperately needed in our churches today.

Let me illustrate what I mean. My first pastorate after I was ordained was my home church, the church in which I had been raised. One morning a deacon made a special trip to the study to talk with me. He said, "Vernon, I can't pray in public. I don't know why, but I can't do it. The fact of the matter is, I can't speak in public either.

Don't ever call on me to speak or pray in public. If you do, I will embarrass you, and I will embarrass myself. I simply can't do either one of these things in public, and I can't seem to overcome the weakness." Tears were in his eyes as he spoke. Then he said, "But anytime anything needs to be done in this church, whether it is to replace a light bulb that has burned out or to put a new roof on the church, you can call on me. I will be glad to do it." Do you know what I did after that? If something needed repairing or remodeling around the church, I would call on him. Sometimes in less than an hour, a whole crew of men would be at the church to work, and that deacon would work right along with them. I learned very early that he was one of the most valuable members I ever had in a church. He was a Haggai. He believed in getting down to business and doing the work that needed to be done. Often I heard visiting speakers and others say, "My, this church is certainly kept up; what a lovely place to come and worship!" Do you know why that church looked so nice? A man in my church could not pray in public. Thank God he couldn't pray in public, because most churches have too many men who love to pray in public. We need people who are working people, too. We need people who are willing to roll up their sleeves and go to work.

Actually, the Book of Haggai is too simple to be in God's Word. It should be a little bit more complicated. Haggai gave the people a sermon. He said, "Go up to the mountain." That is the first point. Then he said, "Bring down the wood." That is point number two. Then he said, "Build a house." That is the third point. Those were God's simple instructions. There was nothing more to say, but there was something to do.

Now God explains why the people of Israel had been having such a difficult time—

✳   Ye looked for much, and, lo, it came to little; and when ye brought it home, I did blow upon it. Why? saith the Lord of hosts. Because of mine house that is waste, and ye run every man unto his own house [Hag. 1:9].

"And ye run every man unto his own house" indicates the zeal and enthusiasm with which they had been taking care of their own interests and building their own homes.

They had been wondering why all of these difficulties had come upon them, but they were too pious to blame God. They claimed that their bad luck was due to circumstances. It was a bad year. "We had a drought, you know," they would say. But God told them, "I want you to know that I caused the drought. I saw to it that you were not successful in your different schemes, and I will tell you why I did it. It is because My house is lying in waste while every man improves his own home."

Let me repeat that the Lord Jesus stated the great principle in the Book of Haggai, which is applicable for all people of all ages, when He said, "But seek ye first the kingdom of God, and his righteousness; and all these things shall be added unto you" (Matt. 6:33). When God is put first in our lives, all other things will take care of themselves. What a message this is! Yet it is so simple, I'm afraid we will miss it.

Therefore the heaven over you is stayed from dew, and the earth is stayed from her fruit [Hag. 1:10].

Naturally, when there was no rain, there were no crops. The wheat and the barley would not grow, and the vines would not produce. God says, "I turned off the spigot; I didn't give you any water."

In our contemporary society we don't interpret life like that. Because we live in a mechanical society, an electronic age, we blame our problems on someone's failure to push a button or on pushing the wrong button. I wonder if God would like to get through to America and say, "Look, has it ever occurred to you that I may be behind the problems you are having? Did it ever occur to you that I am trying to get your attention off things and onto Me?"

Notice that God takes the blame for all of these trials which have come upon Israel—

And I called for a drought upon the land, and upon the mountains, and upon the corn, and upon the new wine, and upon the oil, and upon that which the ground

bringeth forth, and upon men, and upon cattle, and upon all the labour of the hands [Hag. 1:11].

God is saying to them, "Material blessings have been withheld from you because *I* withheld them. *I* am responsible."

In our day, the tendency is to blame first the police—they should have been on the job. Then we blame the mayor, we blame the legislature, and we blame Washington. Very possibly all of them are guilty. But, my friend, has it occurred to you that *you* yourself are to blame? Although we blame men and machines for the conditions of the world, *God* has brought it all to pass. Do you want to blame Him? Go ahead. He told Israel that He was responsible. But He also told them why. They had neglected Him. You see, the solution to our problems is very simple; yet it is complicated. We think that if we put in a new method or a new machine or a new man, our problems will be solved. My friend, why don't we recognize what our problem really is, who caused it, and how it can be solved?

Now Haggai tells us the response to the challenge which God has given to the people of Israel.

CONSTRUCTION OF THE TEMPLE—OBEDIENCE OF THE PEOPLE

Then Zerubbabel the son of Shealtiel, and Joshua the son of Josedech, the high priest, with all the remnant of the people, obeyed the voice of the Lord their God, and the words of Haggai the prophet, as the Lord their God had sent him, and the people did fear before the Lord [Hag. 1:12].

Zerubbabel is the governor, Joshua is the high priest, and "all the remnant of the people" refers to the people who returned to the land of Israel from Babylonian captivity.

Notice that they did two things: (1) They obeyed God. As Samuel the prophet had said to a disobedient king, ". . . to obey is better than sacrifice, and to hearken than the fat of rams" (1 Sam. 15:22). And the apostle John put it this way, ". . . if we walk in the light, as he is in the light, we have fellowship one with another, and the blood of Jesus Christ his Son cleanseth us from all sin" (1 John 1:7). You see, we must walk in the light of the Word of God, and the Word will humble us and show us our failures. A great many of us don't like to have them called to our attention; but if we will recognize them and deal with them, we will find that the blood of Jesus Christ will just keep on cleansing us from all sin, and we will have fellowship with God. So we see that the people of Israel obeyed God.

Also (2) they feared God. The writer of Proverbs says that "The fear of the Lord is the beginning of wisdom . . ." (Prov. 9:10).

It is significant that the leaders of the people, Zerubbabel and Joshua, are mentioned first in their obedience to God. The need today *A JEW* in our country is for obedient Christians in places of leadership. William Gladstone, the famous British statesman, was asked what was the mark of a great statesman. His reply was that a statesman is a man who knows the direction God is moving for the next fifty years. Well, we don't seem to have men in leadership who know the direction God is moving for the next fifty minutes. Oh, how we need men who really know God and are being led by Him!

CONFIRMATION FROM GOD

When they obey God and fear Him, they receive this wonderful confirmation from Him.

> Then spake Haggai the Lord's messenger in the Lord's message unto the people, saying, I am with you, saith the Lord [Hag. 1:13].

He says, "I am *with* you." How wonderful! You remember that the Lord Jesus said to His own, "Lo, I am with you alway, even unto the end of the age." And notice that the promise of His presence rested upon their obedience: "Go ye therefore, and teach all nations, baptizing them in the name of the Father, and of the Son, and of the Holy Ghost: Teaching them to observe all things whatsoever I have commanded you: and, lo, I am with you alway, even unto the end of the world [the age]. Amen" (Matt. 28:19–20). He didn't say that He will be with you if you sit on your haunches and don't do anything for God. He didn't promise to be with you there. He said that He will be with you when you obey Him. That is the place of blessing and of fellowship. And you can't have anything better than that.

Now notice that the leaders enter enthusiastically into the work.

> **And the Lᴏʀᴅ stirred up the spirit of Zerubbabel the son of Shealtiel, governor of Judah, and the spirit of Joshua the son of Josedech, the high priest, and the spirit of all the remnant of the people; and they came and did work in the house of the Lᴏʀᴅ of hosts, their God [Hag. 1:14].**

It is pretty important to see the leadership of the nation in action. Zerubbabel was the civil leader, the governor. He was in the kingly line and was the son of Shealtiel, whose name means "asking of God in prayer." And Joshua, the high priest, was the son of Josedech (Jehozadak) who was high priest at the time of the Babylonian invasion. So we see here the civil and religious leaders joining in with the people in doing the work of the Lord.

This second message was given, and Haggai dates it—

> **In the four and twentieth day of the sixth month, in the second year of Darius the king [Hag. 1:15].**

This is September 24, 520 B.C. The first message, as we have seen, was given on September 1, 520 B.C.—that was when God challenged them. They had responded to the challenge, had come together, had organized the project, were cutting down trees, were making them into lumber, and had started to build the temple. Now, twenty-four days later, Haggai gives them this second message from God, the assurance of His presence.

Haggai was an orderly man, as his book indicates. He was also an administrator. He was a man who was right down to earth. He helped the people rebuild the temple, and as they worked together he continually encouraged and challenged them in their work. The results would be great. God would be pleased, and God would be glorified.

CHAPTER 2

THEME: **D**iscouragement of the people; encouragement of the Lord; appeal to the Law; explanation of the principle; revelation of God's program; expectation for the future

WHERE IS YOUR HEART

In the second chapter we see the discouragement of the people and the encouragement of the Lord. The obvious inferiority of the second temple to the temple of Solomon became a cause of discouragement, but God responded to it.

DISCOURAGEMENT OF THE PEOPLE

In the seventh month, in the one and twentieth day of the month, came the word of the Lord by the prophet Haggai, saying [Hag. 2:1].

Notice that this took place in the seventh month—the previous time they heard God's message of encouragement was in the sixth month. So now they had been working for a month. They had spent about twenty-four days getting organized, and now the temple is beginning to go up. There is great enthusiasm as they see their progress. And they remember God's encouraging, "I am with you."

Now we come to the second item of discouragement.

Speak now to Zerubbabel the son of Shealtiel, governor of Judah, and to Joshua the son of Josedech, the high priest, and to the residue of the people, saying [Hag. 2:2].

This message is directed to the same group of people whom God had encouraged in the previous chapter, the same leaders and the same people.

Now here is the second hurdle which Haggai had to clear as he prophesied to these folk—

Who is left among you that saw this house in her first glory? and how do ye see it now? is it not in your eyes in comparison of it as nothing? [Hag. 2:3].

Many of these who had returned from the Babylonian captivity could remember—although they had been very young at the time—the beauty and the richness of Solomon's temple. This little temple which they were putting up looked like a tenant farmer's barn in Georgia in comparison to the richness and glory of Solomon's temple. Although Solomon's temple had not been a large temple, as temples go, they could remember its ornate richness, the jewels, the gold, and the silver which had been put into it. Before inflation the estimated value of the materials that went into Solomon's temple varied between five million and twenty million dollars—that is quite a difference, of course, but in that day either five or twenty million dollars was quite a sum of wealth. That temple had been like a beautiful little jewel box.

Now let me draw your attention again to the dating of this third message from God: "the seventh month, in the one and twentieth day of the month." If you check this date in Leviticus 23, you will find that it was the seventh day of the Feast of Tabernacles, the final feast of ingathering for the Jews. I am of the opinion that the builders had really pushed and speeded up their building in order to get the temple as far along as possible in order to use it for the celebration of the Feast of Tabernacles. So when some of the old-timers came into it and saw the lack of beauty and richness which had characterized Solomon's temple, they were disappointed. As you know, any kind of structure, whether it is a home or a great office building, doesn't look very impressive before it is completed. You have to wait until the building is finished to really appreciate it. But this little temple in Haggai's day, even when it was finished, was no comparison to Solomon's temple. And there was a mixed reaction to it.

The Book of Ezra, chapter 3:8–13, gives us more background as to what went on at this time: "Now in the second year of their coming unto the house of God at Jerusalem, in the second month, began Zerubbabel the son of Shealtiel, and Jeshua the son of Jozadak, and the remnant of their brethren the priests and the Levites, and all they that were come out of the captivity unto Jerusalem; and appointed the Levites, from twenty years old and upward, to set forward the work of the house of the LORD. Then stood Jeshua with his sons and his brethren, Kadmiel and his son, the sons of Judah, together, to set forward the workmen in the house of God: the sons of Henadad, with their sons and their brethren the Levites. And when the builders laid the foundation of the temple of the LORD, they set the priests in their apparel with trumpets, and the Levites the sons of Asaph with cymbals, to praise the LORD, after the ordinance of David king of Israel. And they sang together by course in praising and giving thanks unto the LORD; because he is good, for his mercy endureth for ever toward Israel. And all the people shouted with a great shout, when they praised the LORD, because the foundation of the house of the LORD was laid."

It may have been just the foundation and a few uprights, but they had to celebrate it. Ezra's record continues—"But many of the priests and Levites and chief of the fathers, who were ancient men, that had seen the first house, when the foundation of this house was laid before their eyes, wept with a loud voice; and many shouted aloud for joy: So that the people could not discern the noise of the shout of joy from the noise of the weeping of the people: for the people shouted with a loud shout, and the noise was heard afar off."

You see, amid all of the shouts of joy there was another sound—a weeping and howling by those who were making a comparison between the two. They were saying, "Look, this little temple that you are putting up here doesn't amount to a hill of beans. In comparison to Solomon's temple, it doesn't amount to anything." This internal criticism was like a wet blanket on the celebration of the construction of the new temple. It dulled the edge of the zeal to rebuild the temple. It poured cold water on the enthusiasm generated by the prodding of Haggai. If you want to dampen a project, all you have to say is, "You think this is great, but you should have seen the original back in the good old days."

When I was a boy, I remember some of the adults talking about the good old days. Well, I don't remember any good old days when I was a boy—those days when I was growing up were hard. I remember the first little church I served in Georgia. It was a little white building sitting on a red clay hill. During my first year there as a student pastor I preached a series of evangelistic messages on the Book of Revelation. I haven't been able to do that again in my ministry, but I did it then, and God blessed. Many young people were saved. On the Sunday night of the final message some of us sat on the steps of the church because it was a warm Georgia evening—most of us were young people—and we were talking about what a wonderful meeting it had been. There was one old man there with whiskers like Methuselah. He said, "You've had some good meetings, young man, but I remember. . . ." When someone starts that, you are headed for the toboggan, and soon you're on the downhill run. He took us for quite a ride down the hill. He told us, "When I was a young man, we really had a meeting here!" As he told us about the meeting, ours seemed pretty small compared to his, although I learned later that he exaggerated a little. Yet what he said was discouraging.

And in Haggai's day the folk, who had been so enthusiastic about the temple they were building, became discouraged.

How is God going to meet this situation? Well, I'll tell you how we in the church would handle it. We would appoint a committee to see what could be done. As someone has said, a committee is a group of people who individually can do nothing and who collectively decide that nothing can be done. Or, as another has said, a committee is a group of incompetents, appointed by the indifferent, to do the unnecessary. Having been a pastor for many years, I am confident that we would use the committee approach to handle this problem. But that is not the way God solved it. He faced the problem squarely and came up with a very simple solution.

> **Yet now be strong, O Zerubbabel, saith the Lord; and be strong, O Joshua, son of Josedech, the high priest; and be strong, all ye people of the land, saith the Lord, and work: for I am with you, saith the Lord of hosts [Hag. 2:4].**

3 TIMES

God's challenge is twofold here. First, He says, "Be strong," three times. He says be strong to the civil ruler. He says be strong to the religious ruler. Then when He speaks to the people, does He have something new for them? No, it's the same thing—be strong. Now that is very simple, but it is very important.

My friend, you and I live in a big, bad world today. What is our encouragement? God's work in many places is small and doesn't seem to amount to very much. What is the solution? Well, here is God's answer to us: "Finally, my brethren, be strong in the Lord, and in the power of his might" (Eph. 6:10). We need to recognize that we can't do anything but that God can do a great deal. Be strong in the Lord. How wonderful that is.

Also in Hebrews 11:34 it says that believers "Quenched the violence of fire, escaped the edge of the sword, out of weakness were made strong . . ." (italics mine). Doesn't God say that He chooses the weak things of the world? God does not choose these big, ornate buildings. He doesn't choose these beautiful mausoleums that have steeples on top of them. Nothing very great is happening in places like that, but things are really jumping in some suburban areas, and many of the smaller churches are packed. I know what I am talking about because I have had the privilege of going across this country several times since I have retired, and this is what I have seen. I have also been abroad several times. I visited one of the great churches in London, England. At one time that church was filled with several thousand people three times a week on a regular basis. When I visited the church on a Sunday night, there were not more than two hundred people in attendance. That great imposing building with its impressive name was not very formidable any more. This same thing is true in my own nation. I have been in some of our great churches, and, my, the amount of lumber I can see in the pews—but nobody is sitting in them. Yet when I go out to some of our small churches, I find that they are packed to the doors and are having two and three morning services.

Today we are to be strong in the Lord. This is repeated many times in the Word of God. Paul, writing to a young preacher, said, "Thou therefore, my son, be strong in the grace that is in Christ Jesus" (2 Tim.

2:1, italics mine). The Epistle of 2 Timothy is Paul's swan song, and in his final message to this son in the faith, he is saying, "You are a son of God. Be strong now." What a word of encouragement that should be.

Somebody says, "My ministry is so insignificant and my group is so small that I don't think it amounts to very much." My friend, if that is what you are thinking, it is the Devil who is talking to you. Don't listen to him. It is God who is going to put the measuring rod down on it and determine who is great and who is not. There are a whole lot of straw stacks being built today, and they look impressive. I myself have always been fearful that I was building a straw stack. Oh, I know there is some gold in it, but have you ever tried to find a needle in a straw stack? How will you find a little piece of gold that is the same color as the straw? God makes it clear that size is not the important thing.

God is saying to you and me, "Watch ye, stand fast in the faith, quit you like men, be strong" (1 Cor. 16:13). Paul wrote this to a bunch of baby Christians over in Corinth. He was urging them to get out of the crib, get out of their high chairs, and grow up. Be strong in the Lord. Oh, how we need that sort of thing in God's work, my friend.

Paul wasn't through with the Corinthians—he wrote a second letter to them in which he said, "(For the weapons of our warfare are not carnal, but mighty through God to the pulling down of strong holds;)" (2 Cor. 10:4, italics mine).

It was my privilege to pastor a downtown church in Los Angeles and to have succeeded some great men. Although I may not have approved of everything they had done, I certainly had great respect for them. They were great preachers. Dr. R. A. Torrey had been the founder of that church. I never walked into that pulpit without first looking to God and saying, "Lord, I am unable, I am insufficient for this task. I call upon You today." I say to you that I am thanking God that out of weakness He can make us strong. For the weapons of our warfare are not carnal, but mighty through God to the pulling down of strong holds. And I told God many times, "Lord, if anything happens here today, You will have to do it because You and I know that this poor boy can't do it at all."

In 2 Corinthians 10:5-6, Paul goes on to say, "Casting down imaginations, and every high thing that exalteth itself against the knowledge of God, and bringing into captivity every thought to the obedience of Christ; and having in a readiness to revenge all disobedience, when your obedience is fulfilled." In other words, make very sure you are being obedient to God. It doesn't make any difference how large or how small the work is. We need to remember, "Be strong." God said to Israel, "Sure, this temple is not as impressive as the other temple was. I know that, but be *strong*. That is my challenge to you." He said three times, "Be strong!"

God's second word of challenge was "and *work*." Just keep at the job. Let God be the One to determine who is doing the greatest work. When we get to heaven and stand in the presence of Christ, I suspect that we will find out that there were people who were greater than Luther in Luther's day, greater than Wesley in Wesley's day, greater than Billy Sunday in his day, and greater than Billy Graham in his day. I used to tell the pastoral staff at the Church of the Open Door, "Someday when we stand before God, He may call some woman to come forward and say, 'This woman was a member of the Church of the Open Door while Vernon McGee was pastor, and she is the most honored one. I am going to reward her.' I'll nudge you fellows and ask if you knew her. You all will say, 'No, we never heard of her.' She is one of the unknown members. All she had was only one little boy. Her husband deserted her, and she raised that boy alone. Then she sent him to the mission field and, my, what a work he did! She was faithful. She didn't have the opportunity to speak to thousands, but she had the opportunity of speaking to one, and that is all God asked her to do." My friend, I think we are going to get our eyes opened in that day when we stand in His presence. He says, "Be strong and work." We are to be faithful at the task which God has given us to do.

Now here is God's glorious word of encouragement: "For I am with you, saith the LORD of hosts."

The fact of the matter is that the *Shekinah* glory had departed from the temple of Solomon long before the temple was destroyed. I have always taken the position that the *Shekinah* glory departed in the days of King Manasseh. He was a ruler who sinned so wickedly that the nation of Israel sank lower than it ever had gone before. If the *Shekinah* glory did not leave during his reign, I can't figure out any other time afterward that it would have been more inclined to leave. If I am correct in this, the *Shekinah* glory, which was the visible presence of God Himself, had left the temple about one hundred twenty-five years before the temple was destroyed by Babylon. Therefore, in Haggai's day, the old men, the ancients, who had seen Solomon's temple, had seen only its outward glory. The *Shekinah* glory had long since gone.

There is no doubt that the outward glory of Solomon's temple was tremendous. As you know, the Mosque of Omar stands on that temple site now, and its dome is gold. I have been told that it is gold leaf. Whether that is true or not, it is really a thing of beauty. I have looked at that dome from the Mount of Olives, and I could have looked at it from Zion. I have looked at it from the tower of a Lutheran church, and I have looked at it from hotel windows—my, how it shines! As I looked at that pagan mosque, I thought of how Solomon's temple must have looked in the bright sunlight of that semidesert air. We know that it was a very ornate, rich temple and that the boards were covered with real gold. How beautiful it must have been! Of course there was no comparison between it and the temple which was then under construction, but God considered Zerubbabel's temple in the different stages of its construction—Solomon's temple, Zerubbabel's temple, and later Herod's temple—as *one* house, not three houses. Therefore it is in the same line as the house (called Herod's temple) into which the Lord Jesus Christ would come. Christ was the *Shekinah* glory. He was God manifest in the flesh. The apostle John said, ". . . we beheld his glory . . ." (John 1:14)—but it was veiled in human flesh. And the Lord Jesus walked into that temple not one time but many times.

So God says to these discouraged builders in the days of Haggai, "Yes, this little temple you are building is not much, but I am *with you.*" My friend, that is a great deal better than having a magnificent temple without God being there. This is the same contrast between that contemporary big church with empty pews—cold, indifferent, and dead—and the little church around the corner packed with people and with a faithful pastor teaching the Word of God. We need to get a correct perspective of what is real and what is not real, what God is blessing and what He is not blessing.

> According to the word that I covenanted with you when
> ye came out of Egypt, so my spirit remaineth among
> you: fear ye not [Hag. 2:5].

Though this new building was not impressive, God says, "My spirit remaineth among you." That was a great deal better than a very ornate temple which was devoid of the presence of God.

This reveals the difference between the ministry of the Holy Spirit in Old Testament and New Testament times. In that day He was among the people. In our day He is in believers. He has certainly changed positions. This is one of the great benefits we have as believers in Christ.

"Fear ye not." If they had no reason to fear, certainly the child of God today should not fear.

DARK AGES 476-1244

QUAKES

> For thus saith the Lord of hosts; Yet once, it is a little
> while, and I will shake the heavens, and the earth, and
> the sea, and the dry land;
>
> And I will shake all nations, and the desire of all na-
> tions shall come: and I will fill this house with glory,
> saith the Lord of hosts [Hag. 2:6–7].

First of all, we need to recognize what God is doing here. He is attempting to get their minds and hearts and eyes off that which is local, that which is very limited, and get their eyes fixed upon God's program for the people of Israel. He wants them to see what is out yonder in the future—extending all the way into the Millennium.

My friend, for us today it is so easy to get the wrong perspective of the Christian life. We get our nose pressed right up to the window of the present, and we don't see anything else. As you know, you can put a dime so close to your eye that it blots out the sun. Well, a dime is like the present that blots out God's plan and purpose for our life. Don't be discouraged because present circumstances are not working out for you. Recognize that for the child of God, ". . . all things work together for good to them that love God, to them who are the called according to his purpose" (Rom. 8:28). That is, "the good," is out yonder in the distance.

"I will shake the heavens, and the earth, and the sea, and the dry land." In other words, God intends to move in judgment. We are going to see, before we finish this little Book of Haggai, that God is looking forward and speaking of the Great Tribulation, which is the Day of the Lord, and later of the coming of Christ to the earth and the setting up of the millennial temple, events which are also included in the Day of the Lord.

"I will fill this house with glory." Although it was a series of houses—Solomon's temple, Zerubbabel's temple (which was torn down by Herod), and Herod's temple—God saw it as one house. And into that temple came the Lord Jesus Christ. The glory was there, although in human flesh. Then Herod's temple was destroyed (even before it was finished) in A.D. 70 by the forces of Rome under Titus. On that temple site no other temple has been built from that time to this. Actually, the Mosque of Omar stands there today, and the Islamic world would never permit it to be removed because it is either the second or third holiest spot in the world of Islam. However, later there will be built the temple which will be designated as the Great Tribulation temple. And after that, the millennial temple will be built on that site. Therefore, seeing it as one house, God says that the day is coming when "this house" will be filled with glory. I believe that the shekinah glory will come with Christ when He returns to the earth. In Matthew 24:30 we read, "And then shall appear the sign of the Son of man in heaven: and then shall all the tribes of the earth mourn, and they shall see the Son of man coming in the clouds of heaven with power and great glory." This verse speaks of the sign of the Son of man in heaven, then immediately speaks of the glory of the Lord. I believe that His glory, the shekinah glory, will be seen in the temple which we designate as the great tribulation temple. But when He comes to occupy it, it won't be a Great Tribulation temple that is in rebellion against Him. There won't be in it the image of Antichrist, but Christ Himself will be present there.

"I will shake all nations." Today it is difficult to believe that there will be more shaking than there has been in the past century. This century was practically ushered in by World War I. That was rather world-shaking. And there have been earthshaking events since then. There was a worldwide depression. There was World War II. Also, oil crises and energy shortages have shaken all nations, but all of these things are nothing compared to the shaking that will come in the future.

"The desire of all nations shall come." The commentators from the very beginning, in fact, the early church fathers, interpreted "the desire of all nations" to be Christ. Frankly, that has disturbed me from the time I was a younger preacher, because I never could believe that Christ was the desire of all nations. There are those who interpret the desire of all nations to be the longing of all nations for the Deliverer, whether or not they realize that the Deliverer is Christ. This may be true, but whom are they going to accept when he comes? They will accept Antichrist. Antichrist is the world's messiah, the world's savior, and they will accept him. I do not think that the nations have any desire for the Lord Jesus Christ.

It is my feeling that the meaning of this passage becomes clear if we continue reading. Now, let's put verses 7–8 together:

And I will shake all nations, and the desire of all nations shall come: and I will fill this house with glory, saith the Lord of hosts.

The silver is mine, and the gold is mine, saith the Lord of hosts [Hag. 2:7–8].

What is the desire of all nations? It is silver and gold. In our day many nations have had to go off the gold standard. When they did this, the economic foundation of the entire world was rocked. Why? Because there still is a desire for gold and silver. When Solomon's temple was built, from five to twenty million dollars worth of precious metals and jewels were used in its construction. It was very valuable. As you read the historical record in Kings and Chronicles, it seems as if Solomon had cornered the gold market in his day. When Nebuchadnezzar cap-

tured Jerusalem, all that wealth was taken away. You may remember
that in 2 Kings 20:12–17 the record tells of ambassadors who came
from the king of Babylon to the king of Judah (which was Hezekiah at
that time), and the king of Judah showed them all his treasures, all the
wealth of Jerusalem. They made note of it, and in due time they cap-
tured Jerusalem and moved all that gold to Babylon. Certainly gold
was the desire of the nation of Babylon, and it is still the desire of the
nations of the world.

"The silver is mine, and the gold is mine." All the silver and gold
in the world belong to God, and there will be plenty of it to adorn
God's house in the future. The future millennial temple will be, I am
confident, a thing of beauty.

*The glory of this latter house shall be greater than of the
former, saith the Lord of hosts: and in this place will I
give peace, saith the Lord of hosts [Hag. 2:9].*

"The glory of this latter house" is, rather, "the latter glory of this
house." Remember that God views the series of temples as one house,
and He is saying that the latter glory of this house, which will be that
of the millennial temple, will be greater than the former. It will be
even greater than Solomon's and certainly greater than the temple they
were then building.

"In this place" designates the temple area as the site of the house
in all of its stages.

"In this place will I give peace, saith the Lord of hosts." I never
visit Jerusalem without going to the temple area. Although I have seen
it at least a dozen times, I still like to go there. Do you know why? It is
because at that spot there will be accomplished what the United Nations and the League of Nations failed to do, which is to bring peace to
the earth. When Jesus Christ comes to this earth, His feet will touch
down on the Mount of Olives, and when He enters that temple area,
peace will come to this earth, for He is the Prince of Peace. He will
bring world peace at that time. The "peace" to which He refers in the
verse before us means finally that.

This peace, however, could also include the peace which He brought at His first coming. At that time He brought peace to men of good will; that is, to men who were rightly related to God. As the apostle Paul put it, "Therefore being justified by faith, we have peace with God through our Lord Jesus Christ (Rom. 5:1). He also brought the peace that passes all understanding, which is for the Christian heart today. He came the first time to bring that kind of peace.

In a day which is yet future He will bring *world peace*, the kind of peace which this world wants and needs.

So the "desire of all nations" is not Christ. I believe that the proper word is *treasure*—the treasure of all nations. He said, "The silver is mine, and the gold is mine," speaking of material treasure. The thought seems to be that the lack of adornment in Zerubbabel's temple would be more than compensated for by the rich treasures which are going to be brought in the day when the millennial temple will be built. Therefore, this passage looks forward to the final days when the millennial Kingdom will be established here on earth. God was encouraging the discouraged builders of Haggai's day to see their temple in the perspective of the ultimate purpose of God.

Oh, that you and I might see our present circumstances in that same way! We need to look at them in the light of eternity and to look at them in the light of God's purpose for us. If God be for us, who can be against us? Hallelujah! Let's not be overcome nor overwhelmed by the circumstances of the moment.

I think of that preacher in Scotland who turned in his resignation at the end of the year. When the elders asked him why, he said, "Because we haven't had any conversions this year except wee Bobbie Moffat." Well, my friend, that discouraged preacher couldn't see that "wee Bobbie Moffat" would become Robert Moffat, the great missionary to Africa, who probably did as much if not more than David Livingstone in opening Africa to Christian missions. That year, which the preacher considered a failure, was probably the greatest year of his ministry. All of us need to see things in light of God's plan and purpose for our lives.

GENTILE —

APPEAL TO THE LAW

In the four and twentieth day of the ninth month, in the
second year of Darius, came the word of the LORD by
Haggai the prophet, saying [Hag. 2:10].

This now, is the fourth message that God gives to Haggai. Notice
again how the dating is geared into the reign of Darius, a gentile ruler,
because there was no king on the throne of either Israel or Judah. The
date is December 24, 520 B.C. The previous message was given in the
seventh month; this message was given in the ninth month.

Thus saith the LORD of hosts; Ask now the priests concerning the law, saying,

If one bear holy flesh in the skirt of his garment, and
with his skirt do touch bread, or pottage, or wine, or oil
or any meat, shall it be holy? And the priests answered
and said, No.

Then said Haggai, if one that is unclean by a dead body
touch any of these, shall it be unclean? And the priests
answered and said, It shall be unclean [Hag. 2:11–13].

You see, on December 24, 520 B.C., Haggai went to the priests and
asked them two questions. Putting it very simply, these are the questions: (1) If that which is holy touches that which is unholy, will it
make the unholy holy? The answer is no. (2) If that which is unclean
touches that which is clean (holy), will the unclean make it unclean
(unholy)? The answer is yes, that is what it will do.

Now these questions are important; so let's get the background before us. There were many facets of everyday life in Israel which were
not covered in detail by the Mosaic Law. There were involved situations and there were knotty and thorny problems which arose in their
daily lives, and there was nothing specific given in the Law which
would adequately cover them. Then how did Israel function under the

RITUAL

Law when there was no specific law to govern certain situations? Well, there is a case in point in Numbers 27 regarding the inheritance of Zelophehad's daughters. The Mosaic Law had made no inheritance provision when a man had daughters but no sons. Zelophehad didn't have any sons, but he had a house full of girls. When their father died, the girls went to Moses and said, "Look here, what about our father's property? The Law says that sons are to inherit, but our father had no sons; he had only girls. So we should have the property." Maybe Moses was not too enthusiastic about this women's lib movement; so he took the matter to the Lord. Well, it is quite interesting to see that the Lord was on the side of the girls. He said, "The daughters of Zelophehad speak right; thou shalt surely give them a possession of an inheritance among their father's brethren." So this took care of that particular question.

God made adequate provision for justice under the Law. This is the way it worked: When a matter arose that was not covered by the Law, they were to appeal to the priests. Deuteronomy 17:8-11 says: "If there arise a matter too hard for thee in judgment, between blood and blood, between plea and plea, and between stroke and stroke, being matters of controversy within thy gates: then shalt thou arise, and get thee up into the place which the Lord thy God shall choose; And thou shalt do according to the sentence, which they of that place which the Lord shall choose shall shew thee; and thou shalt observe to do according to all that they inform thee: According to the sentence of the law which they shall tell thee, thou shalt do: thou shalt not decline from the sentence which they shall shew thee, to the right hand, nor to the left." When a certain situation arose that was not covered by the Law, the people were to appeal to the priest; he would make a decision, and his decision became the law for cases which dealt with the same issue. That was God's method, and it seems to me that we follow this same method today. I once took a course in commercial law, and although I don't remember much of what was taught, I do recall the difference between what is known as statute law and what is known as common law. Statute law is that which is passed by the legislature. When a certain bill comes before that body of lawmakers and is passed, it becomes statute law. That law is written down and stands as law. There are so many statute laws that I am sure no one person knows all of them.

There is also that which is known as common law. For example, a matter is brought into court. Let's say it is the case of John Doe versus Mary Roe. The lawyer for each side of the case looks for a similar case in the books, one that has already been tried, because there is nothing on the statute books that covers that specific issue. So finally they find a similar case that was decided years ago by Judge Know-It-All in Washington. Such decisions which were handed down by courts are known as common law. Therefore, we have two kinds of law: statute law and common law.

And this is the provision God made for Israel. Not every specific case was covered by the Mosaic Law, although great principles were laid down. The priests were to know the Old Testament, and when a case arose which was not covered specifically by the Law, the people were to bring the matter before the priests for a decision. And the priests would interpret the Mosaic Law for the people according to the great principles found in the Word of God.

27 AMENDMENT
To CONSTITUTION

EXPLANATION OF THE PRINCIPLE

Keep in mind that in the Book of Haggai we have come to the post-Captivity period. God's people had already spent seventy years in captivity in Babylon. Only a small remnant had returned to the land, and those people were discouraged. God raised up three prophets to encourage them; and, since Haggai was the very practical prophet, God sent him to the priests to ask the two questions which were not specifically covered by the Mosaic Law.

Remember that when the captives first returned to Jerusalem, they had the enthusiasm to build, but after fifteen years in the debris of Jerusalem and with their enemies outside, they had done nothing about building the temple. They consoled themselves because they had lost their esprit de corps; and sinking into complacency, they were saying, "It's not time to build the Lord's house," and so they did nothing about building it. Haggai spoke into this situation. He encouraged the people; they began to build, and then some of the old- ✱

timers, who had seen the first temple, began to weep and say, "This little temple isn't worth anything." However, for three months the people worked. Then a mercenary spirit entered in, and the people said, "You told us to go to work and build the temple, and if we did, God would bless us. We have obeyed, but God is not blessing us." It was at this juncture that God sent Haggai to the priests with a twofold inquiry. It is actually one question with two facets. Here are the questions and the answers he received: Is holiness communicated by contact? "No," is the answer. The holy cannot make the unholy holy by contact. Holiness is noncommunicable. Is unholiness communicated by contact? "Yes," is the answer. Uncleaness is communicated to the clean by contact. When holy and unholy come in contact, both are unholy. In therapeutics, measles is communicated by contact. In the physical realm, dirty water will discolor clean water—not the opposite. In the moral realm, the evil heart of man cannot perform good deeds. In the religious realm, a ceremony cannot cleanse a sinner.

10 yrs
606
597
586

For God's application of this principle to Israel, we'll have to move ahead to pick up verse 17: "I smote you with blasting and with mildew and with hail in all the labours of your hands; yet ye turned not to me, saith the Lord." God says that when the remnant returned to the land, they didn't turn to Him. They went through the rituals, and they brought sacrifices, and they expected God to bless them, but He did not. Religion, you see, is not a salve you can rub on the outside. Friend, you can swim in holy water, and it won't make you holy. You can go through a ritual, you can be baptized in water and be held under until you drown, but that won't make you a child of God. We sometimes put too much emphasis on a rite. Don't misunderstand me, I think baptism is very important, but it does not impart holiness. It will not change a man's heart.

Now let's look at the second inquiry again: "If one that is unclean by a dead body touch any of these, shall it be unclean?" And the priests gave this answer: "It shall be unclean." Perhaps the key passage that deals with this matter is Leviticus 22:4-6. The Word of God is quite specific. Uncleanness is communicable; unholiness is transferable.

An evil heart cannot perform good deeds. A bitter fountain cannot

1897 Zionism

give forth sweet water. Grapes are not gathered from thorns. Figs do not come from thistles.

There is a syllogism in philosophy where you state a major premise, a minor premise, and a conclusion. In the Book of Haggai the major premise is this: holiness is not communicated. The minor premise is this: unholiness is communicated. The conclusion is that when the holy and unholy come into contact, both are unholy. The Lord Jesus Christ asked the question, ". . . Do men gather grapes of thorns, or figs of thistles?" (Matt. 7:16). As a man thinks in his heart, so is he. An act or a ritual cannot change the heart. A good deed is actually tarnished when an evil heart performs it. This is ceremonial law, friend, but it is applicable to every phase of life—just like the law of gravitation, it is universal.

Let's go into a chemistry lab. I fill two large beakers with water. One container I fill with good, clear, clean water, and the other one I fill with the dirtiest water possible. I begin to pour the clean water into the unclean water. How long will I have to pour the clean water into the dirty water before it becomes clear? I will never make the dirty water clean by pouring clean water into it. What happens when I put one drop of the dirty, black water into the clean water? The clean water becomes unclean. So it is in the material world.

In the world of medicine, how do you cure the measles, and how do you get the measles? Do you take a well boy and have him rub up against the sick boy to make him well? Will that cure the boy with the measles? Of course it won't. What happens? The boy who was well will probably have a good case of the measles.

This principle is also true in the moral realm. The liquor industry gives money to charity, and the race track has a day in which they give all their proceeds to charity. Hollywood produces biblical stories, and we are supposed to applaud them—well, you might applaud, but I won't. The liquor industry can never cover up the awful thing it is doing to human lives by giving a few dollars to charity. Why? Because, when a clean thing and an unclean thing come together, the unclean always makes the clean unclean. May I say to you, young man and young woman, you cannot run with the wrong crowd and stay clean. If you are running with an unclean crowd, one of these days you are going to find out it has rubbed off on you. If you are going to play in the mud, you are going to get dirty.

And this great principle certainly holds true in the religious realm. Most of the religions in the world teach that if you go through their prescribed rituals and ceremonies, you are acceptable to God. However, the Word of God is clear on the fact that going through a ceremony—baptism or any other rite—or doing anything externally will not meet the conditions which God has put down for man.

After all, man's condition is a sad one. We read in Jeremiah 17:9, "The heart is deceitful above all things, and desperately wicked: who can know it?" What a picture this is of the human heart! No one but God can know how bad it is. If we could see ourselves as God sees us, we could not *stand* ourselves. We don't realize how bad we really are. The Lord Jesus made this abundantly clear in Matthew 15:18–20, "But those things which proceed out of the mouth come forth from the heart; and they defile the ear. For out of the heart proceed evil thoughts, murders, adulteries, fornications, thefts, false witness, blasphemies: These are the things which defile a man: but to eat with unwashen hands defileth not a man." Just because you wash your hands, have been through a ceremony, or have performed a ritual does not make you right with God, you see.

I often think of a man I played golf with several years ago in Tulsa, Oklahoma. He told me, "I was a church hypocrite for years. I was a member of a big downtown liberal church. I had been through the ceremonies and had served on every committee. To tell the truth, I was not a Christian, and during the week I was practicing things which no Christian should do. I was a typical hypocrite. Then one day I found out that I was a sinner and needed a Savior. That is the thing that transformed my life." You see, the *heart* must be changed. Listen to the Lord Jesus as He talks along this line: "Ye shall know them by their fruits. Do men gather grapes of thorns, or figs of thistles? Even so every good tree bringeth forth good fruit; but a corrupt tree bringeth forth evil fruit [this is the principle at work]. A good tree cannot bring forth evil fruit, neither can a corrupt tree bring forth good fruit. Every tree that bringeth not forth good fruit is hewn down, and cast into the fire. Wherefore by their fruits ye shall know them" (Matt. 7:16–20). Out of the *heart* proceed the issues of life. The heart must be changed.

Shakespeare had it right when he portrayed Lady Macbeth walking in her sleep, rubbing her little hand, and exclaiming, "Out, damned spot! out, I say! . . . Here's the smell of the blood still: all the perfumes of Arabia will not sweeten this little hand." How true! Neither can all the perfumes of Arabia make the *heart* right with God.

Trying to make yourself acceptable with God through ceremonies and all of that sort of thing is like pouring a gallon of Chanel No. 5 on a pile of fertilizer out in the barnyard in an effort to make it clean and fragrant. My friend, it won't work. The apostle Peter said to Simon the sorcerer, ". . . thy heart is not right in the sight of God" (Acts 8:21). God demands a clean heart. In Ephesians 6:6 God speaks of ". . . doing the will of God from the heart." And in Hebrews 10:22, "Let us draw near with a true heart. . . ." How can a man's heart be made clean when his heart by nature is unclean? Is there something man can do to make his heart clean? No! This is rather like the sign I saw in a dry cleaner's shop in a certain city back East which read: "We clean everything but the reputation." Believe me, that is something you can't get cleaned on earth. The writer of the Book of Proverbs asks the question, "Who can say, I have made my heart clean, I am pure from my sin?" (Prov. 20:9).

Well, God has the prescription: "Come now, and let us reason together, saith the Lord: though your sins be as scarlet, they shall be as white as snow; though they be red like crimson, they shall be as wool" (Isa. 1:18). Peter wrote, "Forasmuch as ye know that ye were not redeemed with corruptible things, as silver and gold, from your vain conversation received by tradition from your fathers; But with the precious blood of Christ, as of a lamb without blemish and without spot" (1 Pet. 1:18–19). One song asks the question, "What can wash away my sin?" That same song answers the question—"Nothing but the blood of Jesus." That is one of the greatest principles ever stated.

God says to the people through the prophet Haggai, "The reason you haven't been blessed is because you have been coming to Me with unclean hands and unclean hearts."

**Then answered Haggai, and said, So is this people, and
so is this nation before me, saith the LORD; and so is
every work of their hands; and that <u>which they offer
there is unclean</u> [Hag. 2:14].**

515 BC

<u>Their unclean hearts made their service for God unclean</u>. This is the
reason that an <u>unsaved person can do *nothing* that is acceptable to
God.</u>

Now, you will find a difference of opinion among Bible expositors
on verses 15–19. Some hold that the verses review the condition of the
returned remnant when they were indifferent to the Lord's house be-
fore they obeyed the Lord and began to build the temple. Other expositors hold that they refer to the people's discouragement *after* they had
built the temple because it had not turned the tide of their misfor-
tunes. Haggai tells them that there has not been time for the change to
work, that evil has an infectious power greater than that of holiness
and that its effects are more lasting.

However, it is my understanding that God is applying to Israel the
great principle of the unclean defiling the clean to illustrate to them
that although they had rebuilt the temple, their *hearts* were still far
from Him, and He was not able to bless them.

**And now, I pray you, consider from this day and up-
ward, from before a stone was laid upon a stone in the
temple of the LORD [Hag. 2:15].**

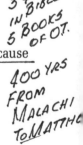
PERSIA
34 TIMES
IN BIBLE
5 BOOKS
OF OT.

He is saying that from this day on He is going to bless them because
now they have turned to Him.

400 YRS
FROM
MALACHI
TO MATTHEW

**Since those days were, when one came to an heap of
twenty measures, there were but ten: when one came to
the pressfat for to draw out fifty vessels out of the press,
there were but twenty.**

**I smote you with blasting and with mildew and with
hail in all the labours of your hands; yet ye turned not to
me, saith the LORD.**

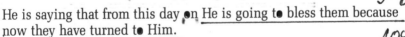
3 BILLION PEOPLE IN
WORLD TODAY

> Consider now from this day and upward, from the four
> and twentieth day of the ninth month, even from the day
> that the foundation of the LORD's temple was laid, con-
> sider it.

Ruth

> Is the seed yet in the barn? yea, as yet the vine, and the
> fig tree, and the pomegranate, and the olive tree, hath
> not brought forth: from this day will I bless you [Hag.
> 2:16–19].

God says, "Now that your hearts are right before Me, I'll bless you." You see, they had rebuilt the temple and had been performing the services of the temple, yet that alone was not enough. In fact, when God had sent them into captivity, they had been going through the temple services. The problem was that their hearts were not right.

My friend, one of the ways that you can make your church a good church—that is, if you have a Bible-teaching preacher—is to go there all prayed up and confessed up and repented up and cleaned up. Then you won't block any blessing that might come to the church that day. Remember that when the unclean touches the clean, what happens is that the clean becomes unclean. Your heart has to be right with God before there is blessing. This is a tremendous principle. I know of nothing more practical.

REVELATION OF GOD'S PROGRAM

> And again the word of the LORD came unto Haggai in the
> four and twentieth day of the month, saying [Hag. 2:20].

"The four and twentieth day of the month" is the same day on which the previous message was given—December 24. On one occasion I was asked why Haggai gave two messages on the same day, and I replied that probably it was because Haggai wanted to go home for Christmas—so he gave both messages before he left. Well, some folk took me seriously, and I received a ten-page letter explaining that in Haggai's day they weren't celebrating Christmas yet! Another letter informed me that no one should ever celebrate Christmas! Well, the fact is that when I don't have the answer to a question, I generally give some facetious answer. And if you won't let this word get out, I'll confess to you that I don't know why Haggai gave two messages on a particular day—but here they are.

> **Speak to Zerubbabel, governor of Judah, saying, I will shake the heavens and the earth [Hag. 2:21].**

"Speak to Zerubbabel, governor of Judah." This message is to the civil ruler, the man in the kingly line of David, and it is God's promise to him.

> **And I will overthrow the throne of kingdoms, and I will destroy the strength of the kingdoms of the heathen; and I will overthrow the chariots, and those that ride in them; and the horses and their riders shall come down, every one by the sword of his brother [Hag. 2:22].**

"I will destroy the strength of the kingdoms of the heathen [the nations]." When God says that He will shake the heavens and the earth and will overthrow the ruling governments, He is speaking of the Great Tribulation period, as He did in verses 6 and 7 of this chapter. He says that He "will overthrow the chariots," because it was that in which the people trusted; in our day it is nuclear weapons. God says, "I am going to remove all of that."

EXPECTATION FOR THE FUTURE

> **In that day, saith the Lord of hosts, will I take thee, O Zerubbabel, my servant, the son of Shealtiel, saith the Lord, and will make thee as a signet: for I have chosen thee, saith the Lord of hosts [Hag. 2:23].**

"In that day"—notice it is not "in this day." It looks forward to the end times. "I . . . will make thee as a signet." The signet was the mark and identification of royalty. A man used it to sign letters and documents. Since it represented him, he guarded it very carefully and usually wore it. It came to represent a most prized possession.

"I have chosen thee, saith the L**ORD** of hosts." As we have seen, Zerubbabel is in the line of David. God's promise is that not only will the Messiah come through David, He will also come through Zerubbabel. Although the name Zerubbabel (Zorobabel) appears in the genealogy of both Matthew and Luke, the one in Matthew is, of course, an entirely different man. God made good His promise to Zerubbabel. The Lord Jesus Christ is just as much the Son of Zerubbabel as He is the Son of David.

The prophecy looks forward to the day when the Lord Jesus will come at the end of the Great Tribulation period. And God intends to put this line of Zerubbabel, this line of David, in the person of the Lord Jesus Christ, upon the throne of the universe. He is the King of kings and the Lord of lords. He will come to the earth to rule. This little Book of Haggai puts Christ in His proper position as the moral ruler, the civil ruler, and the King to rule over this earth in that day, which makes this an important book.

Now it is true that the little temple built in Haggai's day, which became known as Zerubbabel's temple, was not very impressive. But it is very important because it is in the line of temples into which the Messiah Himself will come some day.

Someone has poetically summarized the message of this little Book of Haggai. I regret that I do not know the author, but I shall quote it as we conclude this study—

'Mid blended shouts of joy and grief were laid
  The stones whereon the exile's hopes were based.
  Then foes conspired. The king his course retraced,
His throne against the enterprise arrayed.

And now self-seeking, apathy, invade
  All hearts. The pulse grows faint, the will unbraced.
  They rear their houses, let God's house lie waste.
So heaven from dew and earth from fruit are stayed.

There comes swift messenger from higher court,
　With rugged message, of divine import:—
　"Your ways consider; be ye strong and build;
With greater glory shall this house be filled."

　He touched their conscience, and their spirit stirred
　To nerve their hands for work, their loins regird.
　　　　　　　　　　　　—Author unknown

My friend, again let me say this: Who in our day is going to determine who is doing the great work and who is doing the small work? Your Sunday school class or other seemingly insignificant ministry may be far more important than an impressive work that is well known in our day. Only God can know the importance of it. Let's be found faithful, and then let's work. This is the message of the little Book of Haggai.

BIBLIOGRAPHY

(Recommended for Further Study)

Feinberg, Charles L. *The Minor Prophets*. Chicago, Illinois: Moody Press, 1976.

Gaebelein, Arno C. *The Annotated Bible*. 1917. Reprint. Neptune, New Jersey: Loizeaux Brothers, 1971.

Ironside, H. A. *The Minor Prophets*. Neptune, New Jersey: Loizeaux Brothers, n.d.

Jensen, Irving L. *Haggai, Zechariah, and Malachi*. Chicago, Illinois: Moody Press, 1976.

Tatford, Frederick A. *The Minor Prophets*. Minneapolis, Minnesota: Klock & Klock, n.d.

Unger, Merrill F. *Unger's Commentary on the Old Testament*, Vol. 2. Chicago, Illinois: Moody Press, 1982.

Wolfe, Herbert. *Haggai and Malachi*. Chicago, Illinois: Moody Press, 1976.

TEMPLE: CENTER OF JEWISH
~~HEBREW~~ . WORSHIP

1